HOW TO GIVE A GREAT SPEECH

First published in the United Kingdom in 2010

© 2010 Kolarele Sonaike

The right of Kolarele Sonaike to be identified as author of this work is asserted in accordance with the Copyright, Designs and Patents Act 1988.

ISBN 978-1-4466-3675-6

All rights reserved. No part of this publication may be reproduced, stored in a retrieval system or transmitted in any form or by any means, electronic, mechanical, photocopying, recording or otherwise, without the prior written permission of the author.

HOW TO GIVE A GREAT SPEECH

How to prepare, how to write and how to deliver
a great speech or presentation to wow your audience.

Kolarele Sonaike

For Eva,

who taught my soul to speak.

CONTENT

Introduction ix

<u>How to prepare a great speech</u> 1

1. Stop Writing! 5
2. There are No Rules 9
3. Know your Purpose 11
4. Know your Audience 17
5. Understand the Occasion 23
6. Tell the Truth 27
7. Type, Theme and Tone 31
8. Brainstorm & Research 39
9. Timing 47

<u>How to write a great speech</u> 53

10. The Spoken Word 57
11. Find your Own Voice 63
12. The Title 67
13. Your Opening 71
14. The Introduction 77
15. The Main Body 81
16. Your Conclusion 85
17. Your Closing 89
18. Your Structural Outline 93
19. Writing Tools & Techniques 103
20. Jokes & Humour 109
21. Your First Draft 115
22. Edits & Rewrites 119

How to deliver a great speech — 127

23. Passion — 131
24. Nerves & Fear — 135
25. Delivery Tools & Techniques — 141
26. Notes or Nothing — 147
27. The Venue — 153
28. Aids & Props — 157
29. Anticipating Problems — 161
30. Practice & Rehearsal — 165

Your Speech — 171

Checklist — 173

Author Page — 181

INTRODUCTION

This is how to give a great speech!

This is where to start, where to finish and all the things in between. How to prepare; how to write; and how to deliver.

There are many websites selling off-the-shelf texts and books that promise Churchillian-like speeches with minimal effort; but like all promises of gold in return for peanuts, they are never worth the paper or the HTML pages on which they are written.

Great speeches are unique. They are prepared for a specific occasion, written to suit an individual person and delivered so as to chime with a particular audience. You just won't get that from a pre-prepared download!

To give a great speech requires effort on your part. There is no getting around that. But, do not buy into the myth that you have to be a great political figure, or on the cusp of some great moment in history, to be able to give a great speech, or that there are secrets of public speaking known only to the greatest orators.

There are no secrets. There is no mystery. There are no short cuts or wonder drugs to turn you into a JFK or Barack Obama overnight. What there are, are methods and methodologies, and tools and techniques that work and that tend to feature in most great speeches. The aim of this book is to help you understand and use these things for your own speech.

Giving a great speech does not require complex levels of oratorical skill, or years of dedicated training. On the contrary, you need only understand a series of relatively straightforward steps, and then do the hard work of implementing them.

Great speeches are given every day by ordinary men and women alike. They do it not by magic, but by application; not by accident, but by careful design.

Great speeches start revolutions, kick-start companies, soften hearts, win elections, quell riots, land jobs, broaden minds, secure investments, win over in-laws and save lives. Clients are impressed by a great presentation and are more amenable to doing business as a result. Protesters are energized by passionate orators and are more likely to act, rather than just talk. Electorates are swayed by eloquent pitches and are more likely to actively vote, rather than just silently support.

Even when the goals are not so lofty or the stakes so high, a great speech still brings great rewards. You will notice that you are more respected than before; people are more receptive to you than they once were, and doors that were previously shut, suddenly open up. You will bask in the warm glow of your audience's approval, even its adoration, and for some time afterwards, all things will seem possible.

You can and will give a great speech if that is what you want to do.

You just have to be prepared to work for it.

How to use this book

Using this book is straightforward. You can start from the beginning and work your way through to the end, or you can pick and choose just the bits that you need. It is up to you.

The book is divided into chapters that each represent a stage of the speechmaking process and each stage is divided into four parts:

i) A quote or phrase that encapsulates the overall message of that stage

ii) 'The Purpose': a short explanation of the purpose of that stage, i.e. the reason it is a necessary part of the speechmaking process

iii) 'What you need to know': a detailed explanation of what you need to know about that stage

iv) 'What you need to do': a checklist of the specific steps you need to take to cover that stage

You will find some references to the great speeches and speechmakers of history, but these are meant only as illustrations of good principles. Do not be put off or intimidated by them. Remember that most of these great speechmakers struggled as much as we all do with public speaking, and often had dedicated speechwriters and coaches to help them with the things you will learn in this book.

This book is meant to help and not to hinder. So, if you disagree with, or simply do not find anything in it useful, then discard it. But do so only after careful consideration and not just because there is work involved.

How to Give a Great Speech is a comprehensive, nuts and bolts guide to the art and science of successful speechmaking. It aims to work for every speechmaker at every level of speechmaking ability, and for any and every occasion on which a speech has to be given, however long or short, trivial or important.

It won't tell you what to say, but it will help you with how best to say it.

The rest is up to you.

Best of luck!

Kolarele Sonaike

GREAT SPEECH.CO
THE 'GREAT SPEECH' CONSULTANCY

HOW TO PREPARE
A GREAT SPEECH

HOW TO PREPARE A GREAT SPEECH

Proper preparation is crucial if you want to give a great speech, because the most common reason for bad speeches the world over, is the failure to prepare.

Think of preparation as you do the foundations of a house. If you do not lay them properly, or at all, your house will collapse. Taking time to prepare may seem like wasted time when you could simply be writing the speech itself, but there is truth in the adage that *'proper preparation prevents poor performance'*.

It is during the preparation stage that you will work out the aims of your speech; the truth at the centre of its content, the type of audience you are addressing and how best to address it, the optimum length for your speech, the nature and spirit of the occasion and the best theme and tone to use.

Even if you fancy yourself a great natural raconteur, consider the instructive words of Mark Twain (one of the most naturally gifted speakers of his generation):

"It usually takes me three weeks to prepare a good impromptu speech."

STOP WRITING!

'Pens down, please!'

THE PURPOSE

> The purpose of this section is to stop you making the biggest mistake that is also the most common cause of bad speeches the world over. Writing before you prepare. Penning without planning.
>
> This section will help you understand the importance of avoiding the fatal trap of starting to write too early.

WHAT YOU NEED TO KNOW

This is how to give a bad speech:

Wake up the day before the speech is due to be given in a blind panic; grab a pen and paper and start writing; surf the Internet for some jokes; shoehorn in phrases or passages you have had in mind for some time and that are simply too good to leave out; have a sleepless night worrying about the day to come; write and rewrite the speech right up until the last minute and then step up to the microphone in a blind sweating panic; deliver the speech far too quickly, speaking for far too long, and to no one in particular; finally sit down to consolatory applause from an audience as relieved as you are to be done with one of the most painful passages of time in recent memory.

If any, or all of those steps sound familiar, the chances are you already have, or are about to give a bad speech, or at the very least a lesser speech than the one you are capable of.

The key to good speechmaking is PREPARATION, PREPARATION, PREPARATION!

Therefore, the first step to giving a great speech is to stop yourself from writing anything at all until you have gone through the full preparation process. More than that, if you have already written anything before proper planning, tear it up now before you get too attached to it. It will never be as good as what you will come up with once you have properly prepared.

There is no specific amount of time that you must set aside to prepare, before you start writing. In truth it is a question of how long you personally need. Generally, the more time you allow the better, but you should avoid taking too long so that you lose momentum and the process becomes stale.

One rule of thumb is to allow one hour (to prepare, write and practice delivery) for every one minute of your speech. In any event, however much time you do devote to your speech, you

should divide that time equally, so that you use:
- One third of your time for preparation of your speech
- One third for writing your speech, and
- One third to practice delivery of your speech

Even if you are called with only 30-minutes notice to give a speech, you should still divide this time equally; one third each for preparation, writing (or making notes) and then practicing delivery (even if this is just a run-through in your head).

Ideally, all phases of the speechmaking process (preparation, writing and delivery rehearsal) should be completed at least one day before the due date for the speech, allowing your subconscious the time and space to contemplate and refine the finished product and to give your speech the edge. JFK only added the famous 'Ich bin ein Berliner' line moments before actually delivering the speech, showing the value of giving the mind enough time to think about a subject before final delivery.

But for now, just stop writing! There will be more than enough of that later on.

WHAT YOU NEED TO DO

- Stop writing and tear up or delete anything already written before you become too attached to it.
- Allow 1 hour (for preparation, writing and delivery practice) for every 1 minute of your speech.
- As a general rule of thumb, allocate one third of whatever time you have to preparation, one third to writing and one third to delivery practice.
- Leave enough time to prepare and, ideally, plan to complete all steps (including preparation, writing, delivery rehearsal) at least 1 day before the due date for delivery of your speech.

THERE ARE NO RULES

'Rules are made to be broken'

THE PURPOSE

> The purpose of this section is to stop you slavishly following any so-called 'Rules' when giving your speech.
>
> Certainly, there are tools and techniques, methods and methodologies that help, but nothing (including anything stated in this book) should be treated as a 'Rule', because in speechmaking there are no absolutes.

WHAT YOU NEED TO KNOW

There are no 'Rules'!

A number of books on speechmaking will expand at length about 'Rules'. One will insist you speak from memory; another that you write out every word. Some suggest making a point only once; others that you should repeat everything. Some say use proper diction; others recommend speaking colloquially. Dress up vs. dress down. Use Power Point vs. speak without notes.

For almost every 'Rule' that says one thing, you will find a 'Rule' that says the opposite. But the truth is there are no 'Rules'; if by 'Rules' they mean something to be followed and adhered to at all times and in all circumstances, no matter what.

Your sole aim is to give a great speech, and your audience will not care whether a particular 'Rule' was followed if the resulting speech is poor. Equally, it will not fault you for breaking a 'Rule' if the resulting speech is excellent. There is nothing that you must, or that you must not do, when giving your speech. There are things that tend to work and things that usually don't. Whether you describe those things as 'Rules', guidelines or principles or, as this book calls them, tools, techniques and methods, the point is they are meant to serve and help you, not restrict or imprison you.

Use what works, ignore what doesn't! Your aim is to give a great speech, not to follow 'Rules'.

WHAT YOU NEED TO DO

- Treat all so-called 'Rules' as nothing more than guidelines or techniques to be followed if they work for you, and discarded if they don't.

KNOW YOUR PURPOSE

'Know your Goal!'

THE PURPOSE

> The purpose of this section is to ensure that you are clear about the objectives for your speech, because you need to know where you are headed, before you can work out how to get there.

WHAT YOU NEED TO KNOW

What do you want to achieve? This is the central question to ask and answer to yourself for any speech you give, because it will determine how you prepare, write and ultimately deliver your speech.

For every speech there is a *specific* goal, a *general* objective and a *personal* motive. These are the purposes of your speech. They are the things you want to have accomplished by the end of your speech.

Specific Goal

The *specific* goal is the direct and obvious purpose of your speech. It is what your speech is most obviously about; the ostensible reason that your speech is being given.

For example, if you were a scientist giving a speech about a new advancement in the treatment of cancer, your specific purpose might be to explain all the details of this new treatment to your audience, or it might be to denounce the new treatment and expose it as flawed. If you were giving a best man's speech, your specific purpose would probably be to tell the wedding party a little about the groom, in an entertaining way.

Your specific purpose should always be kept at the forefront of your mind as you prepare, write and deliver your speech, because if your speech does not achieve at least this purpose, it will have been pointless.

General Objective

The *general* objective of your speech is your wider aim. This is distinct from your *specific* purpose because it represents your indirect, but larger goal.

The achievement or not of this objective is the clearest gauge of whether or not your speech was successful.

For example, if you were the head of a software firm giving a speech, your specific purpose might be to unveil a new programme just developed, but your general purpose would be to show consumers and investors that your firm is the most innovative computer company in the world. If you were a head teacher speaking with the specific purpose of persuading parents to donate money for a new swimming pool, your general purpose might be to show that the school remains an excellent one and good enough for their children.

Your general purpose is the true aim of your speech. Unlike your specific purpose, you don't necessarily talk directly about it, but it is what your speech is *really* about.

Personal Motive

The *personal* motive is your personal aim or agenda for your speech. It is what you want to achieve for your own personal satisfaction; the impression you want your audience to have about you by the end of your speech.

So, if your specific goal is to introduce the main speaker at a political rally, and your general objective is to energize the crowd, your personal motive might be to show the audience that you are the natural successor to that main speaker (Barack Obama used this to great effect in his 2004 Democratic Convention speech, introducing the then-Presidential candidate, John Kerry).

These three purposes, specific, general and personal, are the focus of your speech. They can be described as what your speech is about (specific goal), what your speech is really about (general objective), and what your speech is really, *really* about (personal motive).

It is important to identify only one of each of these purposes for your speech; that is, only one overall specific, one general and one personal purpose. This is because however long, detailed and brilliant your speech is, your audience will always only come away with one overall impression about your speech specifically and generally, and about you personally.

This does not mean your speech must be simplistic, or that you cannot tackle complex and difficult subjects. On the contrary, your speech can be as nuanced and technical as necessary with various sub-goals and reference points, etc. However, these must all fit within the clear and defined context of your overall purposes; otherwise the speech will simply have no focus.

For instance, political speeches during election campaigns often have to appeal to a huge audience, cover masses of detail and explain many issues; yet the great political speeches are still the ones that have a clear, overall specific purpose (e.g. to justify the party's manifesto policy on crime), a clear, overall general purpose (e.g. to show that the electorate should vote for that party) and a clear, overall personal motive (e.g. to show the electorate that the politician can be trusted).

When working out your purposes, your thinking should be:

"If there is one thing I want the audience to take away from my speech specifically, generally and about me personally, what would it be?"

Any further sub-goals should be consistent with these overall goals. If they are not, discard them; otherwise you risk giving a speech that has no real focus.

You should also ensure that each purpose is very clearly defined. To do this, make sure you can state your specific, general and personal purposes in one sentence each, of no more than 15 words per sentence.

Once you know what you are trying to achieve, you are much more likely to actually achieve it!

WHAT YOU NEED TO DO

- Work out the specific purpose of your speech. Write it out in one sentence of no more than 15 words.

- Work out the general purpose of your speech. Write it out in one sentence of no more than 15 words.

- Work out the personal purpose of your speech. Write it out in one sentence of no more than 15 words.

- Work out and write down any other goals or aims you have for the speech, and examine them carefully to ensure they do not detract from, or undermine the pursuit of the main goals. If they do, dispense with them!

KNOW YOUR AUDIENCE

'Who's there? What do you want?'

THE PURPOSE

> The purpose of this section is to ensure that you know exactly who your audience is, and how best to speak to it, so as to ensure that you achieve the purposes (specific, general, personal) that you have set out for your speech.

WHAT YOU NEED TO KNOW

A speech is only great if it works with your intended audience. So, your aim must be to connect with your audience when you give your speech.

A brilliantly nuanced and complicated speech that goes over the head of a down to earth audience is a bad speech. It doesn't matter that your turn of phrase is ingenious and your ideas incredibly ground-breaking, if your particular audience doesn't *'feel'* it, your speech will have failed. For example, if you were an inventor speaking at a scientists' convention, you might talk in detail about the steps you went through to create your invention, the challenges you worked your way around, etc. This might well interest fellow scientist greatly. However, if you were describing the same invention, but to potential commercial investors, you would be better advised to talk about the unique marketability of the product, cost of production, the sale value etc, as this is more likely what such an audience would be interested in.

So in preparing for your speech, it is imperative that you know your audience so that you will then know how to write and ultimately deliver your speech in a way that connects with it.

Fortunately, however many people make up your audience and however diverse their backgrounds, opinions, etc., you can still treat your audience as one single entity. The reason is this: Once individuals become a crowd and then an audience, they take on a common identity and share a common opinion. This is no doubt due to our psychological need as human beings to be social and bond with others. You will find that the audience laughs and cries as one, applauds or boos largely as one. Even if, once separated, no two individuals within that whole audience will have exactly the same opinion about every part of your speech, whilst they are part of a group or an audience, they will fuse together and generally act and react in a uniform manner.

It is this one body that will ultimately judge your speech, and so it is to this one body that you must direct your speech. This has the added benefit that you can avoid trying to be too many things to too many people at once, which will just turn your speech into a poorly focused ramble.

Therefore, you need to gain as much knowledge and understanding as you can about your audience to enable you to customise your speech to that particular audience. You should consider:

- Who exactly is your true audience?

  Is it everyone physically in front of you at the time of the speech? Is it a few key individuals within that group of people in front of you? Is it people watching on television, or listening on radio? Is it consumers, voters, the media, etc?

- What are the facts and demographics about that defined audience?

  How many people will be in the audience? What is the audience's age range, gender ratio, wealth status, race, religion, nationality, cultural and social origin, language ability, level of education and intelligence, political persuasion etc?

- What are the general views and opinions of your audience?

  What are its likes and dislikes, hopes and fears, wishes and expectations? What secrets or shared beliefs or experiences do the members of the audience have that you can tap into?

- What is your audience's level of knowledge and familiarity with your speech topic?

  What does it already know and think generally about your speech topic? This will help you decide the appropriate level of detail you need in your speech.

- What is the view or opinion of your audience about the specific, general and personal purposes of your speech?

    For example, if your specific purpose is to motivate your audience to join in a sponsored walk to raise money for your charity, you need to know if your audience is open or resistant to such physical exertion, so that you can pitch your speech appropriately.

    If your personal motive for your wedding speech is to show how much you love your wife, but you know that the bride's side of the family doubts this, your speech will have to contain the right amount of loving sentiment to convince the audience otherwise.

The more information you have about your particular audience, the better you will be able to tailor your speech to that audience and connect with it. But the information you gather must be relevant to your speech topic, such that it will make a difference to the way you will write and deliver your speech.

Do not waste time gathering irrelevant information.

For instance, investigating and finding out your audience's religious views is unlikely to help you if you are giving a speech about how best to grow vegetables in a home garden; or if you are giving a presentation about the future prospects of a business, knowing your audience's racial origins will probably have little, if any, impact on your speech. Whereas, if you are looking for investment from venture capitalists in a new start-up company, it will help to know the level of their wealth or the kind of prior investments they have made so, you can pitch accordingly; if you are speaking at a mosque about the dangers of radicalism, you would be wise to determine if you will be faced with young, disaffected and angry men, or world-weary widows, who have suffered enough loss.

Knowing the number of people in your audience will help you gauge the level of formality you will use when delivering your speech (the smaller the audience generally the less formal your speech style will need to be); knowing your audience's age range may help you avoid references that will be unfamiliar to your audience (no sense reminiscing about the joys of vinyl to members of the iPod generation).

So, be smart and discerning in the information you gather to avoid wasting time and energy on irrelevance.

Getting to know your audience will help you work out how it thinks and feels and will make it much more likely that you will give a speech that says the right things in the right way so that your audience connects with you and your speech.

WHAT YOU NEED TO DO

- Treat your audience as one single body or entity; focusing on its common views, opinions, etc.
- Decide who precisely your audience is.
- Find out as much about your audience as you can, including its demographics, general views, feelings and opinions. Restrict what you seek to find out about your audience to only those matters that are relevant to your speech topic and the way you will write and deliver your speech.
- Find out your audience's current view of the specific, general and personal purposes of the speech.
- Work out what level of knowledge and familiarity your audience has with your speech topic, as this will help you determine the level of detail you should use in your speech.

UNDERSTAND THE OCCASION

'What's the Occasion?'

THE PURPOSE

> The purpose of this stage is to ensure you take the time to understand the nature of the occasion on which you are to speak, so that you can ensure that your speech complements the spirit of that occasion.
>
> It is when the speech and the spirit of an occasion are perfectly aligned that something great happens.

WHAT YOU NEED TO KNOW

Every occasion is unique. Every occasion has an essence or a spirit.

It is the common feeling; the mood of the moment, that thing in the air – however you describe it. It is there on every occasion on which a speech is to be given, and a great speech is the one that perfectly complements that spirit.

More than anything, your audience will have an emotional response to your speech, because it is not what you say, but how you make them feel, that your audience will remember, and this emotionality is directly related to the spirit of the occasion and the extent to which your speech harnesses that spirit.

This may sound abstract, but it is important to understand.

In Earl Spencer's famous eulogy to his sister, Princess Diana, his words were carefully chosen to reflect the mood of boiling anger felt by the public at the circumstances of the Princess's death and her troubled relationship with the Royal Family. His speech was acclaimed because it tapped into and expressed the mood of the moment to his chosen audience.

Similarly, Enoch Powell gave his famous 'Rivers of Blood' speech at a time when there was deep fear and insecurity generally, amongst the indigenous British population, about the effects of mass immigration into Britain.

These speeches had a high level of 'synergy' with the mood and spirit of the occasion on which they were given, and this contributed hugely to the success of those speeches.

So, if you are the Father of the Bride at a wedding, with obvious tension between the two families, a speech that somehow addresses or takes account of this feeling, may have the best chance of achieving greatness.

If you are giving a speech about your company's performance to shareholders when business prospects are low, the market weak and competition strong, a speech that tackles this mood intelligently is much more likely to be acclaimed than a speech that simply ignores it.

If you are a preacher, sermonising about a multiracial society, you should understand whether the prevailing mood is one of hope for the benefits of diversity, or fear for the social changes that such multiculturalism brings, or both, so that you can be the spiritual guide that your congregation is looking for.

Hopefully, you will simply be able to sense the mood or spirit of the occasion, because it is there around you. But, in any event, you should ensure that you know:

- The basic facts of the occasion; i.e., what kind of occasion it is – a business conference, protesters' rally, school assembly, political debate, wedding, science fair, etc.

- What the prevailing mood of the occasion is for your audience; whether it is a time of hope or fear, peace or violence, energy or apathy, change or stability, growth or decline, joy or sadness, proactivity or indifference, interest or boredom, positivity or negativity, love or hate, etc.

Knowing this information will help you work out how best to tailor your speech to the occasion.

For instance, if you are addressing a small workshop for business start-ups during a recession, the prevailing mood might be one of fear and uncertainty; whereas for a speech at the same time to a large convention of venture capitalists, the prevailing mood for that audience might be one of opportunism; i.e., the potential to profit in times of uncertainty. If the occasion is the celebration of your father's 80th birthday, it might be a time of genuine joy, perhaps mixed with respect and awe at the success and achievements of the man; or it might be joy but tinged with sadness because his time is short due to illness.

Imagine yourself as a historian trying to describe, for posterity, the occasion on which your speech was given. Apart from the facts about the venue, audience, location, etc., how would you sum up the occasion in one line?

The important thing is to discover and ensure you appreciate that intangible spirit, because you have to tap into this when you give your speech.

Your aim is to give a speech that your audience feels captured the moment.

WHAT YOU NEED TO DO

- Work out the essence or spirit of the occasion on which your speech is to be given by considering:
  o The basic facts of the occasion
  o The prevailing mood of the moment for your particular audience
  o Or alternatively; imagine you are a historian looking back trying to describe the occasion on which the speech was given, in an editorial. What words would you use to capture the spirit of the occasion?

TELL THE TRUTH

'And the Truth shall set you free'

THE PURPOSE

> The purpose of this section is to ensure you understand the importance of finding and telling the 'Truth' in every part of your speech.
>
> The 'Truth' in a speech is what resonates with your audience and is an essential component of every great speech.

WHAT YOU NEED TO KNOW

'Truth' is the single most important ingredient of every great speech!

It cuts to the heart of the listener. It is what every audience, whether consciously or unconsciously, longs to hear from every speaker - whether it is a great 'Truth', a trivial one, humorous or devastating. 'Truth' is what we relate to when we see a great acting performance, or listen to a great singer. Their performances feel real and authentic, and in the context of speechmaking it is 'Truth' that hooks an audience, making it listen attentively.

But 'Truth' in the context of speechmaking is not absolute or universal; rather it is entirely relative to your audience's point of view.

For instance, it may be true for an audience of teenagers that old people are boring, but this will obviously not hold true for an audience of pensioners. An audience of stockbrokers may buy into the philosophy that 'greed is good', but this won't be the case for charity workers.

Your speech should tell the 'Truth' at all times, so you need to know what that 'Truth' is for your audience. In particular, you should know or work out:

- What the 'Truth' is for your audience about the specific goal you have for your speech (your specific purpose)
- What the 'Truth' is for your audience about the wider objective for your speech (your general purpose)
- What the 'Truth' is for your audience about your personal agenda for your speech (your personal purpose)

So your personal agenda may be to show your staff that you have recovered from a bout of illness and are now fit to lead them, but if the 'Truth' for your audience is that you still seem unsteady, then you need to know this so you can be as persuasive as you need to be in your speech.

Even if your aim is to challenge the perceived 'Truth' on a topic, you still have to work with that 'Truth', rather than against it. However radical or shocking you wish your speech to be, the steps taken to get there must be grounded in the 'Truth' from your audience's point of view; otherwise your speech will simply not succeed.

In her famous 'Freedom or Death' speech, Emmeline Pankhurst of the Suffragettes spoke about the need for equal rights for women, which went completely against the conventional opinion of the day. However, she won over her audience by building up to that conclusion through a series of 'Truths' that the audience could accept; namely that women were also human beings, it was the universal right of any human being to oppose an unjust law, that in politics it is those that make the most noise that are heard, etc.

In the 16th century when Queen Elizabeth I stood before her troops to rally them before battle, she acknowledged the perceived 'Truth' of the time that women were inferior to men with the words, *"I know I have the body but of a weak and feeble woman"* but she went on to overcome that 'Truth' with the stirring words, *"but I have the heart and stomach of a king."* By working with, rather than against the 'Truth', the Queen inspired and boosted her troops' morale as well as any man or King could have done (which was her general purpose).

For every point you are going to make (however important or minor) in every part of your speech, you must ask yourself – "Is this the 'Truth' for my audience?"

Of course, telling the 'Truth' is not without risk. If you get it wrong, you could damage your prospects of achieving your speech's purposes. You may even bring trouble on yourself for doing so. So, you may find it easier to gloss over the 'Truth' so as not to offend. This is obviously your choice. But, understand this. If you do not speak the 'Truth' to your audience, you may be able to give an average or perhaps even a good speech, but you will not give a great speech.

How you use the 'Truth' and incorporate it into your speech will be worked out during the writing phase. You may choose to be subtle and diplomatic, or blunt and brazen. You may use humour to soften the 'Truth', or show passion and anger about that 'Truth'.

But for now, commit to seeking out and speaking the 'Truth' about your speech topic, and about every issue in your speech.

WHAT YOU NEED TO DO

- Commit to speaking the 'Truth' (from your audience's point of view) in every part of your speech.
- Work out what the 'Truth' is for your audience about your specific, general and personal purposes.
- Even if you are planning to challenge the 'Truth' for your audience, ensure that the steps leading up to your challenging conclusions are grounded in things that are 'true' from your audience's point of view.

Work with the 'Truth', rather than against it.

TYPE, THEME AND TONE

'What's your type? Set the theme. Watch your tone!'

THE PURPOSE

> The purpose of this stage is to ensure that you work out the type of speech you are giving, the best theme for your speech (bearing in mind your audience, the occasion and your purposes) and finally, the most appropriate tone to use in giving the speech.

WHAT YOU NEED TO KNOW

Type – is the kind of speech you are going to give.

Theme – is the overall message or impression you want to leave with the audience about your speech topic.

Tone – is the overall message or impression you wish to leave with the audience about you personally.

<u>Type</u>

There are basically 4 different types of speech. Speeches to:
i) Inform or explain
ii) Persuade or advocate
iii) Motivate
iv) Entertain

The informative or explanatory speech is given to inform or explain a subject to the audience.

The persuasive or advocatory speech is given to persuade the audience to adopt a certain point of view, or to advocate for that view or conclusion.

The motivational speech is given to motivate the audience to do something.

The primary focus of an entertainment speech is to entertain the audience, but such speeches are in fact very rare, since most speeches will have a more specific aim or focus, but use humour or entertainment to achieve that aim.

Whilst most speeches may have elements of two or more of these types, there is always one primary or dominant type, and you must be clear from the outset what that type is.

The best man's speech is usually given to inform the wedding party about the groom (even if it is also meant to be entertaining). The business presentation is often given to advocate for a product or service (even if it is also often designed to inform generally about the company). The political activist seeks to motivate the masses (even if much of the speech will be about persuading the audience to adopt a point of view).

Understanding the type of speech to be given is the first step in working out the content of the speech.

For instance, a speech to inform will have to focus on setting out the necessary facts and supporting explanation, whilst a speech to motivate will give the facts that are necessary, but will focus more on stirring emotions to motivate the audience to act. A speech to entertain has to focus on the humour, whilst a speech to persuade may use humour to get the audience onside, but its main focus is the conclusion it wants the audience to reach.

Knowing the type of speech being given therefore also stops you wasting time and words on things that are more relevant to a different type of speech.

The type of speech most obviously mirrors your speech's specific purpose. So, if the specific purpose of your speech is to tell the history of your family, the type of speech you are giving is an informative one. If your specific purpose is to get people to shop in your store, the type of speech you are giving is a motivational.

Theme

The theme of your speech represents the overall message or impression that you wish the audience to be left with about your speech topic.

Within minutes of its conclusion, your audience will have forgotten much of the detail of your speech and within days it will have forgotten 90% of it.

Think of Martin Luther King's famous 'I have a dream' speech.

How much of the detail of that speech could you actually recount? Most people will only remember the one phrase, 'I have a dream'. A few may be able to recite three or four lines. Only the tiniest minority would be able to repeat more than 10% of the speech and probably only because they studied it; this, for possibly the most famous and most referenced speech in history.

What audiences do remember is what the speech was about overall and, in particular, their feelings about the speech. This is because the theme of the speech (about the need for freedom and equality for all) was so clearly set out.

Take Churchill's mighty 'We shall fight on the beaches' speech. Most British people will only remember the specific phrase, 'we shall fight them on the beaches... we shall never surrender...' Yet, almost all will be clear on the overall message of the speech, which was about Britain's resilience, unyielding resolve and determination. This was because Churchill established that theme strongly during the conclusion of his speech.

Your theme is most closely related to your general purpose, which is your wider objective.

How to work out your theme

Consider your general purpose, which is your overall grand objective, and decide what the one message or overall impression is which you wish to leave with your audience about your speech topic; i.e., if there was one thing about your speech that you would want the audience to remember, what that one thing would be.

So, for instance, if your general purpose is to encourage the audience to donate to your charity, then the one thing you might want your audience to remember is how dependent charities are on people's generosity. This might then lead you to adopt a theme about 'the virtue of giving' so that the overall message that the audience takes away with it, is that yours is a cause worthy of support.

If the specific purpose of your speech is to tell the Olympic committee about your Olympic plans, and the general purpose is to persuade the Olympic movement to give the hosting of the Olympics to your city, the theme of the speech could be, 'unity that sport creates and how your city embodies this principle'. Sebastian Coe used this theme to great effect in his successful pitch on behalf of the London 2012 Olympic bid.

A useful technique for working out a theme is to think of it as a one-line slogan or hook, in the same way that companies identify themselves with slogans.

Tesco projects itself as the cheapest supermarket with the hook, 'Every little helps!'
L'Oreal encourages its customers to pamper themselves with their products with the hook, 'Because you're worth it!' Nike imprints its message of action and energy with the tagline, 'Just Do It!'

The theme (much like a hook or slogan) says everything about your speech in one simple sentence. It is the one thing you want your audience to remember about your speech long after it has forgotten the detail of the speech itself.

Tone

The tone of your speech is the impression you want to project to the audience about yourself. It is the one thing you want your audience to remember about you personally.

It is therefore most closely related to your personal purpose (what you want to achieve for yourself through your speech). Your tone is how you influence the audience's impression of you.

For instance, if you are a groom and your personal motive is to prove to your new parents-in-law that you are not as irresponsible as they fear, a tone of dignity or seriousness is better than one of playfulness.

If you are a CEO and your personal purpose is to dispel fears that you do not have the stomach to fight to save the company, you might adopt an overall tone of passion or love for the company. On the other hand, if people think you are too headstrong without being strategic, the more appropriate tone would be one of calm, clear-headedness.

There are an infinite number of different tones for a speech: light-hearted, serious, funny, passionate, fiery, calm, resolute, sad, happy, grave, agitated, determined, humble, statesmanlike, apologetic, impatient, magnanimous, etc. The point is to find one that fits with your personal purpose, and conveys the impression about yourself that you want it to convey to your audience.

<u>Choosing a complementary type, theme and tone for the speech</u>

Your type should match your specific purpose. Your theme should match your general purpose, and your tone should match your personal purpose. All these should work together as a coherent whole.

Imagine that at the end of the speech, two audience members are discussing your speech. What would they say? What would be their overall impression of you and your speech?

For example:

For a speech by a team leader to her staff, two staff members might afterwards have a discussion along these lines:

JOHN: What do you think?
SARAH: Convincing. (Type of speech – persuasive)
JOHN: She's right, you know, we've just got to hang in there. (Theme – perseverance)
SARAH: What about her?
JOHN: She seems to really believe in the company. (Tone – I'm in it with you)

For the political activist, two members of the crowd might say:

TUNDE: What do you think?
FOLA: He definitely wants us to get involved, doesn't he? (Type – motivational)
TUNDE: He's right that we've been through worse. (Theme – we shall overcome)
FOLA: Yeah, and he never seems to give up. (Tone – I'm up for the fight (determination)

Your speech will no doubt contain a number of different points, ideas, imagery, etc., but remember that it is always one overall impression and feeling about you and your speech that your audience will take away with it.

If you want to give a great speech, you have to control that impression and feeling, and you will do this by using the right type, strong theme and appropriate tone in your speech.

WHAT YOU NEED TO DO

- Decide what type of speech you are giving. Is it to entertain, inform or explain; to persuade or advocate, or to motivate? This should relate to the specific purpose of your speech.
- Decide one overall theme for your speech. This should relate to the general purpose of your speech. It is the one thing you want your audience to remember about your speech topic.
- Decide one overall tone for your speech. This should relate to the personal purpose of your speech. It is the one thing you want your audience to remember about you personally.

BRAINSTORM & RESEARCH

'Know more than you show!'

THE PURPOSE

> The purpose of this section is to ensure you work out every point that could be made on the subject of your speech (even if most of those points will ultimately not make it into your final draft).
>
> A speech should ideally only contain about 10% of your total knowledge of the speech topic. But, it should be the best 10%!

WHAT YOU NEED TO KNOW

The best speeches are the ones where the speechmakers are experts on the topic. They seem to be totally up to speed with the subject matter, giving the impression that they could talk endlessly on the subject if needed, but have chosen to give their audience only the best bits.

This is your aim for your speech – to be a complete master of your subject matter but to treat your audience to just the best parts of what you know; and you do this through proper brainstorming and research.

It is hard work!

You may be tempted to skip this part altogether. But, this is definitely a stage that will reward your efforts now, with the hugely positive benefits it brings during the actual writing phase.

Brainstorming is the process of working out all the facts, thoughts, issues and ideas relevant to the subject of your speech, and then putting them into a useful order that will help you to pick out the parts that will work best for your speech. It is the moment when you allow your mind to drift and wander; thinking laterally, vertically, logically, abstractly and in whatever other ways necessary to bring out every conceivable point that could be made on the topic.

A great speech should only ever use 10% of the total knowledge of the speaker on a chosen subject. This means that if once you have written your speech, you find that you have actually used more than 10% of your total knowledge, you probably did not brainstorm enough in the first place.

There is no set way to brainstorm. Some will keep a pad close by and jot down points continually. Others will mind-map. Some will start from the broad picture, gradually narrowing down to the specific; others will think totally randomly.

It really is a question of what works for you.

The important thing is that, through your brainstorming process, you should work out as comprehensive and complete a list of points about the speech topic as is possible for you to have. Look at everything from every angle and try to gather varied points and ideas not just many points along the same lines. Consider the six primary elements of any story and speech – what, who, where, when, how and why:

- What (*What* is it? *What* could it be? *What* did he do? *What* will it take? Etc.)
- Who (*Who* did it? *Who* is involved? *Who* is going to benefit? Etc.)
- Where (*Where* did it happen? *Where* are we going? *Where* is it now? Etc.)
- When (*When* did it happen? *When* is she going? *When* will we win? Etc.)
- How (*How* is it going to be achieved? *How* did he do that? *How* is she feeling? Etc.)
- Why (*Why* did they do that? *Why* does this happen? Etc.)

Research is a key stage in the brainstorming process. For every point you identify for your speech, you should research properly until you have as much detail as you need.

Again, there is no set way to research.

You can pick other people's brains; there are books, newspapers, TV, radio, Internet, the library, encyclopedias, Google, Wikipedia, etc. Information is readily available in this day and age.

If you are giving a best man's speech, as well as using your own knowledge of the groom, gather information from friends and family, work colleagues, teachers, the fiancée and previous partners. Consider his star sign, his grandparents, historical events on the day of his birth, anything and everything.

If you are giving a business presentation about efficiency savings that need to be made, you should know everything there is to know about the business; its sales, costs, staff morale, inner workings, prospects, markets, competition, consumers, etc.

Having researched fully to complete the brainstorming stage, you could go further and group these points into a workable order.

Again, this is hard work, but if you are prepared to do it now, it will make things easier later on.

i) Place all your points under the category of the purpose they are most relevant to; i.e., specific, general or personal purpose – this allows you to see whether you have sufficient points that you are able to make, in order to achieve each of your purposes.

ii) Secondly, put the points in order of importance within those categories – this will help you later, when you come to sift through all your points, to choose the best stuff that will actually make it into your speech.

For example, for a Business Presentation to potential investors about a new product: **Type of Speech**: To advocate

GENERAL	SPECIFIC	PERSONAL
To promote the company as worthy of investment	To showcase a new product	To show I am the best CEO to lead the company
• Profit margins are excellent • Dividends will be paid this year • Competition is	• Product is original and patented • Second phase due in a few months	• Personal passion for the company • Vision for the future of the company

	• Will tear strips off the competition	• History of having led other companies through worse
weak		

Example: Wedding – Best Man's Speech
Type of Speech – To Inform

GENERAL	SPECIFIC	PERSONAL
<u>To liven up a wedding</u>	<u>To tell the wedding guests about the groom</u>	<u>To express depth of friendship to the groom</u>
• Great venue • Father of the bride was champion marksman so groom should be careful • Bridesmaids look great	• Never lets friends down • Totally smitten by bride • Mistakenly arrested for criminal damage	• Carried me down mountain when leg broken skiing • Lent me money • My best friend

Example: Demonstration Rally
Type of Speech – To motivate

GENERAL	SPECIFIC	PERSONAL
<u>To show the resolve of the anti-war movement</u>	<u>To get people to march against a war</u>	<u>To establish myself as the leader of the movement</u>

• Thanks to the huge numbers that turned up • Acknowledge international support • No violence reported	• War is illegal • Human cost is massive • Money could be better spent elsewhere	• I started the first petition against the government • My mother protested against Vietnam war • I have been arrested several times for protests

Example: Introduction of Main Speaker at a Science Forum
Type of Speech: To inform

GENERAL	SPECIFIC	PERSONAL
<u>To warm up the audience</u>	<u>To introduce the main speaker</u>	<u>To get into the speaker's good books (so he will consider me as research assistant for his next project)</u>
• Joke – how many scientists does it take to change a light bulb • Give big round of applause • This is a time when scientists are badly needed	• Nobel prize-winner • Best-selling author • Only gives 1 speech a year	• Express personal admiration for him • His book made me take up science • Named first child after him

Do as much work now as you have the stomach for.

Remember, the more work you put in at this stage, the easier and more enjoyable you will find the writing phase of your speech.

WHAT YOU NEED TO DO:

- Write down every point that occurs to you that is relevant to your speech.

- Try to gather varied points and ideas, rather than lots of points along the same lines.

- Research comprehensively so that you have sufficient detail for your speech. Aim to know so much that only 10% of your total knowledge on the subject will actually make it into the speech.

- Place every point into the category of purpose to which it is most relevant; i.e., specific, general, personal.

- Place each point in order of importance within those categories.

TIMING

'Less is most definitely more'

THE PURPOSE

> The purpose of this section is to ensure that you work out the right length for your speech, so that it is not too short or too long.
>
> The best speeches feel short. The worst speeches feel too long.

WHAT YOU NEED TO KNOW

The most common speechmaking crime is speaking for far too long.

It is the greatest complaint that audiences have about speeches, yet it is also completely avoidable. A well-planned speech will allow you to achieve your speech purposes in the shortest possible time and with the least number of words because there has never been an audience that complained because a speech was too short.

Think about the length of some of the greatest speeches in history.

- Abraham Lincoln's Gettysburg address – 271 words
- Churchill's 'We shall fight them on the beaches' speech – 307 words
- JFK's 'Ich bin ein Berliner' speech – 694 words
- Barack Obama's 'Yes, we can!' speech – 1,210 words
- Martin Luther King's 'I have a dream' speech – 1,651 words

At a mere 16 minutes, Martin Luther King's speech was the longest. How many mind-numbingly dull speeches, with limited content and of minimal importance, have you heard that push beyond 30 minutes, for no particular reason?

Of course, it may be that there really is a need to cover substantial amounts of material in your speech. Political speeches and business presentations (for example) often need to tackle a wide range of topics and issues, and so are unavoidably lengthy, but can be no less brilliant.

So, the issue is not so much the length of the speech, but the economy of the words used. The best speeches always leave the audience wanting more and so seem shorter than bad speeches, which always seem to take forever.

Therefore, if there is one 'Rule' when it comes to speechmaking (and of course there isn't), it is surely this: Less is more. Shorter is always better!

How to work out the timing and length of your speech

i) First, decide how long you want your speech to be. This will either be a length of your choosing, or a time slot that you are given.

Whatever time you initially decide on, consider again whether the speech really does need to be that long. Think about how long a 5-minute, 10-minute, 20-minute, 1-hour speech actually feels to the audience, and this should encourage you to reduce your time.

ii) Secondly, work out the number of words a speech of that length will amount to.

The average speed for a speech is between 100 – 165 words per minute, depending on the speed of talking, audience response, etc. Therefore, a 10-minute speech will use between 1,000 – 1,650 words; a 30-minute speech will use 3,000 – 4,950 words, etc.

However, this is only a guide. You need to work out your own word-per-minute average. To do this, simply read out a set text (ideally another speech) over a three-minute period as close as possible to your normal delivery style and pace. Then, take the number of words you get through and divide by 3 to arrive at your natural word-per-minute rate.

Try to anticipate and factor in things like audience response. So, if there is likely to be lots of applause, or laughter points in your speech, work out how long your speech will be halted for, to allow the applause or laughter to pass.

iii) Once you have your words-per-minute average and the proposed length in minutes of your speech, this will give you the total number of words at your disposal for your speech.

So, if your speech is to be 7 minutes long and you speak at 135 words per minute, the total number of words for your speech is 135 x 7 = 945 words.

This may seem overly formulaic, but it is the simplest way to ensure your speech will be the right length. Be wary of simply assuming that you will magically write and deliver a speech of the right length without properly planning for it. It is the easiest thing to speak for far too long, and audiences hate it above all else.

The force of a speech is usually inversely proportional to its length. So, the shorter the better; the longer, the less impact.

Plan your speech length carefully and keep it short.

WHAT YOU NEED TO DO

- Find out or set the ideal length of your speech in minutes, making it as short as possible.
- Work out your average speech rate in words-per-minute (and adjust as necessary to allow for audience response and interaction.
- Multiply that average number of words-per-minute by the length of time of your speech to give you the total number of words you will have for your speech.

CONGRATULATIONS!

You have now completed the crucial preparation stage, which means:

- You are a Master of the subject of your speech, knowing everything there is to know about it.
- You are clear on the type of your speech, your overall theme and general tone.
- You know exactly how long you are going to speak for, and how many words this will take.
- You have clearly defined your specific, general and personal purposes.
- You understand that 'Truth' is the single most important quality your speech must have, and are committed to finding and speaking the 'Truth' in every part of your speech.
- You know exactly who your audience is, what it already knows about your speech topic and its current view of your speech purposes.
- You are clear on the spirit of the occasion and that your speech must tap into this.
- You know that there are no speechmaking rules that you must follow at all costs, only techniques and principles that should be used if they work for you.
- You have torn up anything you have already written before properly preparing for your speech, to stop yourself being emotionally tied to it.
- You know to leave sufficient time to properly prepare, write and rehearse your speech.
- You are determined to keep your speech short.

Even if you have only completed some, but not all, of these stages due to lack of time, interest or motivation, your prospects of giving a great speech are already far better now than they were before.

Keep going!

HOW TO WRITE
A GREAT SPEECH

HOW TO WRITE A GREAT SPEECH

Writing your speech after proper preparation is like building your house, having laid strong foundations. You have to capitalise on your good beginnings and create something that is carefully constructed and well balanced.

The good thing about speechwriting is that you do not have to be a great writer to write a great speech. A speech is nothing more than a conversation with your audience. So, if you can hold a good conversation, you can write a great speech.

But, it takes effort and commitment. You will need to outline, write and rewrite your speech, possibly several times, before you get it just right. At the start this may feel mechanical, almost artificial, as you work your way through, trying to put the right words in the right order to make your speech work. Eventually though, your speech will come alive, and start to flow. This is when your speech turns from a work of science into a piece of art that moves people.

You have it in you to write a great speech. You just need to make the effort.

THE SPOKEN WORD

'Keep it Simple!'

THE PURPOSE

> The purpose of this section is to ensure that you understand the difference between the written word and the spoken word, so that when you come to write your speech, you do so for the benefit of an audience that will hear your speech, and not for a reader that will read it.

WHAT YOU NEED TO KNOW

To be able to write a great speech you first have to understand the difference between the spoken word and the written word.

The spoken word is created to be heard. The written word is created to be read.

They are two entirely different forms of communication and you must respect the difference, or you will fail to engage with your audience on the right level. A text that sounds great on paper will often fall flat when delivered as a speech. Therefore, a speechmaker should focus not on how well a speech will read, but on how well the speech will sound.

If you were to transcribe the text of a great conversation you had with a friend, what you would probably notice is that it was full of 'ums and ers', repetition, circularity, grammatical and syntax errors, incomplete and semi-coherent sentences, etc. Yet, it was still a great conversation.

Or take the lyrics of a great song. When sung they can be incredibly moving and profound, but on paper those same lyrics are often simple, even banal. Consider, for instance, the lyrics to the Beatles' moving song, 'Yesterday'. Certainly, they are profound and poetic, but as far as the language itself goes, it was pretty basic stuff.

With Churchill's famous 'We shall fight on the beaches' speech, he concluded with the stirring passage:

"We shall fight on the beaches, we shall fight on the landing grounds, we shall fight in the fields and in the streets, we shall fight in the hills; we shall never surrender!"

Powerful words, but the language itself is very simple. No great lyrical or literary ability was required to write it. There is no clever configuration of abstract syntax; just easy, direct words and phrases using the simple technique of repetition for emphasis (discussed later). The language involved could probably have been written by almost anyone with a fairly basic grasp of English. Still, it was a great speech!

The key to great speechwriting is simplicity.

Written texts can afford to be extravagant and full of literary nuances, but the words of a great speech are simple, even simplistic; using straightforward, plain language.

No matter how deep or complex the issues, the mantra to repeat to yourself when writing your speech is, 'Keep it simple'. You are having a conversation with your audience so you need to speak in a way your audience will understand.

Sentences should be short (on average 15 words or less). You should make only one point per sentence, and avoid long and elaborate sentence construction, which are difficult for an audience to follow.

Words and phrases should be uncomplicated; the kind of words you use in your own conversations.

This is not because the audience is simple and unintelligent – far from it. Audiences have a great capacity to take in and understand even the most complex topics, but unlike readers, who can linger over a passage in a book and read and reread it as often as they want, your audience will generally get to hear the words of your speech only once, and in real time. If the language is not straightforward so that the audience can concentrate on the content itself, you will lose that audience's attention.

So, the novelist may write, 'The perspective of the patron is sacrosanct,' but your business presentation should just say, 'The customer is always right.' The writer might write, 'Our eventual triumph is assured,' but your political rally speech should just say,

'We shall overcome!' A newspaper obituary column may state, 'Michael Smith's reputation as a man of substance was unimpeachable,' but your eulogy should just say, 'Everyone who knew him, thought Mike was a great guy!'

Grammar that is suitable for speechmaking is also very different from the grammar that is appropriate for written texts. You can speak 'posh' or 'cockney', the *'Queen's* English' or *'pidgin* English' if this works better for your particular audience. You can misspeak, be repetitive and break every rule of the language without affecting the quality of your speech.

This gives you as a speechmaker a great advantage, because it means you do not have to be a great writer to be able to write a great speech. You also do not have to be a great man or woman, or be on the cusp of some great moment in history, to be able to give a great speech. It does not matter that you are not a Mandela or a Gandhi, or that you do not have the turn of phrase of Shakespeare.

The great speeches of history were great, not because of the fanciness or complexity of their language, but because, amongst other things, they:

- Spoke the 'Truth' to the audience
- Complemented the spirit of the occasion
- Served the purposes for which the speech was given
- Showed a clear understanding of the audience
- Had a clear theme and tone
- Showed the speechmaker's mastery of the speech topic
- Followed or broke the 'Rules' of speechmaking as necessary
- Were concise, using an economy of words
- Used simple, direct language that people could understand

In short they did all the things we have already looked at through the course of this book, whether this was by deliberate design, or natural instinct. This means that if you know all those things about your own speech, you have as much chance of giving a great speech to your audience as those great speechmakers did to theirs.

And, best of all, you only need a basic understanding of language to be able write it.

Just keep it simple.

WHAT YOU NEED TO DO

- Commit to writing a speech that sounds good to an audience, rather than reads well to a reader.
- Follow, or ignore, rules of grammar, syntax, etc. as work best for the audience.
- Keep it simple. Commit to using simple language to present the content of the speech (no matter how complex that content).
- Use no more than 15 words on average per sentence.
- Make one point per sentence and avoid long, elaborate sentence constructions that are difficult to follow.

FIND YOUR OWN VOICE

'Be true to yourself!'

THE PURPOSE

> The purpose of this section is to help you work out your own individual style of voice so that when you come to write your speech, you will be able to do so in a manner that will suit you.
>
> No matter how technically great a speech is, if it is not written in a style that complements you as a speechmaker, it will not make for a great speech.

WHAT YOU NEED TO KNOW

Your speech must be tailor-made for you, or it will not make for a great speech.

It may be full of remarkable insight, excellent content, side-splitting humour, but if it is not written in a way that suits your own unique style of voice, it won't work.

Imagine a brilliant solo part written for a violin, but played on a tuba. It just doesn't sound quite right.

No sense writing grandiose, eloquent phrases with elaborate analogies, if you are a no-nonsense, straight-talking kind of guy. You wouldn't write the same speech for George W. Bush as you would for Barack Obama! Equally, it is missing a trick to write a speech that is slow and deliberate, if you are a passionate spitfire. Gandhi was a softly spoken Hindu, small in stature, but with a large intellect. His style of speech was accordingly understated, well-reasoned, yet intellectually aggressive. By contrast, Hitler was a ferocious firebrand with a ruthlessly direct mentality. His speeches were mesmerising because of the power of his oratory, and his speeches were written in a style that allowed this power to shine through.

So, you must be clear on what kind of speechmaker you are. It is impossible to set out all the different styles of voice that exist, but there are some common ones and most people fit into these common categories:

- Direct, calm and logical – Gandhi, Mandela
- Passionate and emotional – Malcolm X
- Entertaining/humorous/natural storyteller – Sir Peter Ustinov, Mark Twain
- Eloquent and grandiose – Barack Obama, JFK, Margaret Thatcher, Martin Luther King

Do you speak quickly or slowly? Loudly or quietly? Aggressively or calmly? With a high voice or low voice? Are you naturally funny or serious? Do you have an easy accent or difficult twang? Do you pay attention to detail, or focus on the bigger picture? Do people respect you or fear you, or both, or neither? Do people instantly warm to you or do they find you cold? Do you convince people with passion or logic, etc?

Work out your own natural style so that you will be clear to write in a way that suits you, using words and phrases that will sound right when spoken by you. If you can, ask a good friend to give you an honest opinion.

If you are a natural storyteller, when you come to write your speech, you may use lots of anecdotes to illustrate your points; whereas if you are an emotional and passionate speaker, you may want to rely primarily on the force of your argument and structure the points in a way that allows you to build up momentum.

If you are good at telling jokes and have good timing, you may use humour to sugar-coat your content. If you are more serious, you may prefer to tackle the issues head-on. If you are one for calm logic and detail, you may win the audience over with calm and logical detail; whereas if you are naturally eloquent, you may look to carry the audience away with great imagery.

Understanding your style of voice and keeping it in mind when you are writing your speech, will help you tailor-make your speech to suit yourself.

WHAT YOU NEED TO DO

- Work out your natural style of voice and commit to writing your speech in a manner that specifically suits you.

THE TITLE

'What's in a name?'

THE PURPOSE

> The purpose of this section is to help you devise a title that sends the right signals about your speech to the audience.

WHAT YOU NEED TO KNOW

The speech title is often the first thing the audience will know about your speech and as such, it represents an opportunity to make a good first impression.

Even if your audience will not be aware of the title, it helps to create one anyway, as this will help you focus your mind on the message and specific direction of your speech.

Most titles are mundane, adding little if anything to the speech itself. But this is a missed opportunity. A great title is like the label on a bottle of wine. It should sell the speech to the audience, by drawing in the audience. Ideally, it should:

i) Reflect the specific purpose of the speech.
ii) Capture the audience's interest or imagination.

Reflect the Specific Purpose

The title should reflect the specific purpose of the speech; i.e., what the speech is ostensibly about.

If the specific purpose of the speech is to launch a new model of a car, the title should make this clear. If the specific purpose is to argue in favour of abortion, the title should say so in some way.

The audience, on hearing the title, should then know what the coming speech will be about.

Capture the Audience's Interest or Imagination

The title should be captivating, so that it already sets the audience wondering about the speech to come. Instead of straight, obvious and dull, the title can be quirky, explosive, challenging, inspiring, dynamic, off-key, etc.

In 1959 physicist, Richard Feynman, gave an incredibly technical speech on the subject of nanotechnology to the American Physical Society, but titled the speech, *'There's Plenty of Room at the Bottom'*. Before he even spoke the audience was buzzing in anticipation. Dale Carnegie's best-selling book, 'How to win friends and influence people', immediately grabbed people's attention and made them want to find out more, purely because of the unusual title.

Proper audience analysis will ensure that the title chosen is captivating and interesting to your particular audience.

Your title should sell your speech to the audience, as a book cover sells a book to prospective readers.

WHAT YOU NEED TO DO

- Choose a title to your speech that:
    - Tells the audience what it is about to hear
    - Reflects the specific purpose of the speech
    - Is captivating and interesting or intriguing to the particular audience
    - Sells the speech to the audience, making it want to listen

YOUR OPENING

'You had me at hello'

THE PURPOSE

> The purpose of this section is to ensure that you understand the importance and purpose of the Opening of your speech.
>
> A good Opening engages the audience from the start and sets it up to receive the rest of the speech.

WHAT YOU NEED TO KNOW

Every speech will obviously have:
- A beginning
- A middle, and
- An end

This falls in with the famous motto about speeches that you should "tell them what you're gonna tell them, tell them, and then tell them what you just told them".

But, more accurately, almost all speeches will follow the basic structure of:
- An Opening – the first thing you say to your audience
- An Introduction – the proper beginning of the main part of the speech
- A Main Body – the detail and substance of the speech to support your eventual conclusion
- A Conclusion – the finale/climax setting out your conclusions
- A Closing – the last thing you say to your audience

The Opening of your speech is critical. It is the very first thing you will say to your audience. It is your honeymoon period and is when your audience is at its most interested and receptive. As with the Opening sequence of a movie, or the first few bars of a song, an audience always gives a speechmaker the benefit of its complete attention for a very short, but crucial period. This short period cannot be wasted.

With a good Opening the audience is set up to receive the rest of the speech and you have the chance to go on to give a great speech. Whereas a bad Opening will almost inevitably lead to a bad speech, because once lost from the start, an audience is almost impossible to recover.

This makes your Opening the most significant part of your speech – not necessarily for the content, but for its purpose and impact. So, whilst your Opening may include the customary

'Good Morning, Ladies and Gentlemen' or other such standard greetings, you should consider whether in fact you can dispense with this or at the very least give your Opening more substance than just this.

With your Opening you can be as creative and innovative as you wish, as long as the goals of the Opening are achieved, which are:

- To engage with and establish a bond with your audience.

- To set the general tone for your speech (i.e., the impression of yourself that you wish to give the audience). Your Opening will give your audience its first impression of you, so this is the best place to establish your chosen tone

As long as these goals are achieved, you can open the speech however you wish.

Methods of Opening are unlimited and you should use this lack of constraint to your advantage to make your Opening interesting. Tried and tested methods include:

- Shocker

   A surprising, even explosive Opening will grab the audience's attention immediately. This can be anything from a physical demonstration (standing on a table), to letting off a banger, or even just shouting out a bold or controversial statement. The point is to shock the audience or to challenge its expectations.

- Quotation, saying, proverb

   A relevant quotation, saying or proverb that encapsulates your theme is also a strong Opening. The audience is immediately presented with something familiar, to which it can relate, even if the substance of the speech itself will be new. Quotes from Shakespeare and other great writers, celebrities and public figures, religious books, proverbs, etc., all have this quality. Altered quotations and proverbs can also work well; that is, taking a well-known text or saying and changing its words to suit the needs of the speech; e.g.;

All is fair in love and *Business*', or, 'If you can't stand the heat, get someone who can', etc.

- Anecdote

An anecdotal story or account, that is relevant to the topic of the speech, is a very useful tool for drawing an audience into a speech. It is a story that indirectly in some way illustrates the theme of the speech, which will be developed through the rest of the speech. The anecdote, as with every other part of the speech, must have the ring of 'Truth' to it for your audience. It can be an anecdote about anything; from something personal (a reference to a childhood experience), to something completely impersonal, but still relevant (an adapted fable, cartoon story, etc.).

- Question

Posing a question that will then be answered through the course of the speech is a very direct technique to hook the audience straight into the topic of the speech, and often used in persuasive or motivational speeches.

- Humour

Humour must be truthful, and have purpose and relevance to the speech topic (see the section on jokes & humour). Starting a speech with a joke, or a humorous story, presents a great opportunity to get your audience onside.

- Statistics

Statistics that illustrate the focus of the speech are particularly useful for informative or persuasive speeches. Used intelligently they can bring the subject of the speech into sharp focus. They should be relevant and as far as possible, made personal to really connect with your audience (see Writing Tools & Techniques later).

- Location

Referring to the location of the speech is one way of flattering and relating to an audience; 'Last time I was here in Lagos...' etc., followed by an interesting anecdote about the city that leads the audience into the speech.

- Date

    Every day of the year has historical significance, and a historical event that happened on the day of your speech, can often be worked into the Opening of a speech. Wikipedia has an excellent tool for finding out what happened on a particular date in history, as does the BBC website 'On this day' section. Again, this must be relevant to the speech and not just an interesting, but random and unrelated event.

Basically, there is no limit to the kind of Opening that can be used. The important thing is to ensure that the Opening draws in the audience, rather than alienating it, or worse, leaving it indifferent.

An Opening can be low-key or high-impact; either way it must engage! It must grab them at hello!

By way of analogy, if a speech is like a meal, the Opening represents the initial aperitif (even before the starter), the first taster that signifies the start of something great to follow.

WHAT YOU NEED TO DO

- Understand that your Opening needs to:
    - Engage with and help to establish a bond with the audience.
    - Set the general tone for your speech (i.e., how you personally want to come across to your audience).
    - Make your audience interested in the rest of the speech to come.
    - Be relevant to the rest of your speech.

THE INTRODUCTION

'And now for the moment you've all been waiting for'

THE PURPOSE

> The purpose of this stage is to ensure that you understand what the Introduction of a speech is for, and why it is important.
>
> The Introduction forms the first part of the substance of your speech. Its purpose is to introduce the audience to the Main Body of the speech, where the substantive points will be made.

WHAT YOU NEED TO KNOW

Whilst your Opening is the very first thing that you will say to your audience, the Introduction forms the first part of your speech proper.

The purpose of the Introduction is to lead your audience towards the main points of the speech to come, which will be made in the Main Body.

The Introduction is usually, but not always, where you will set out the intended direction of your speech. This can be done by actually outlining the points that will be made through the course of the speech, or by focusing only on the general theme that will be fully developed through the Main Body of the speech.

So, for the *informative* speech, you might make a statement setting out the issue or topic that you are going to explain to your audience; i.e., *'The purpose of this speech is to...'*, or *'How do you solve the problem of...'*, or *'Today, I'm going to talk to you about...'*. For a *persuasive* speech, you could set out the dilemma or dispute that you are going to try to persuade your audience about. For the *motivational* speech you might set out the problem that requires action or remedy. Finally, for the *entertaining* speech, you might start the beginning of the main humorous story.

There is no set way in which an Introduction must be written, as long as it serves its primary purpose of preparing the audience for the main part of the speech.

Using the meal analogy, the Introduction of a speech is equivalent to the starter of a three-course meal. It must whet the audience's appetite so that it is salivating by the time the main meal comes along.

WHAT YOU NEED TO DO

- Understand that the purpose of your Introduction is to lead your audience towards the Main Body, where the detail of your speech will be given.

THE MAIN BODY

'With my body, I thee honour'

THE PURPOSE

> The purpose of this section is to help you understand the objectives of the Main Body of your speech, that it is the most difficult part of the speech to get right, and by far the most common point at which bad speeches fail.
>
> But, get it right, and the resulting speech will be excellent.

WHAT YOU NEED TO KNOW

The Main Body of your speech is the heart of your speech.

This is where the detail needed to establish your overall message must be set out, and where you will make all the points necessary to achieve your speech purposes (specific, general and personal). It is the most important point of your speech and where great speeches excel and bad speeches fail.

With great speeches, the Main Body is written entirely with a view to the conclusions that will be reached later. With bad speeches, the Main Body has no focus and gets lost in detail without any specific direction; things are said for the sake of it, rather than for a specific reason or purpose.

The Main Body of your speech is also the point from which the audience will no longer give you the benefit of any doubt, or any unearned attention. So, the most important goal for your Main Body is to keep your audience engaged and interested as you move towards your Conclusion.

To do this you must ensure that the Main Body of your speech has Direction, Momentum and Variety.

Direction – Your audience must feel that you know what you are doing and where you are going; that you are deliberately taking it from one point to the next towards an eventual destination, rather than talking haphazardly with no particular aim or goal in mind.

If the audience feels that you are rambling, or heading nowhere in particular, it makes the speech seem longer. Then, instead of concentrating on what you are saying, your audience drifts through the speech praying for the moment it eventually ends.

Momentum – The greatest engine of momentum comes from

economy of words. Every point should be made with the least number of words necessary; i.e., concisely.

<u>Variety</u> – This is also important so that your speech does not feel monotonous or one-dimensional. To give the Main Body variety and keep the audience interested, it should move from light to heavy touches, funny to serious, general to specific, angry to light-hearted, etc. It should avoid simply making the same point in lots of different ways, but should instead make lots of varied points that each have a different element or focus.

Ultimately, the aim is that by the end of the Main Body of the speech, all the detail you need to give your audience to support your coming Conclusion has been given, so that when you do move on to your Conclusion, it makes sense to the audience.

The Main Body of your speech will also have to be written, keeping in mind those factors already looked at, namely:
- Your audience
- The 'truth' at the heart of your speech
- Your type, theme and tone
- Your specific, general & personal purpose
- Your overall message
- The spirit of the occasion
- The length of your speech (in time and words)
- Your natural style of voice

Using the meal analogy, the audience must be fully fed by this main course, so that it feels it has gotten its 'money's worth'.

WHAT YOU NEED TO DO

- Understand that the Main Body of your speech:
  - Is the heart of your speech.
  - Will need to have direction, momentum and variety.
  - Is where all the points that need to be made, must be made, so as to achieve the specific, general and personal purposes of the speech, leading compellingly to the speech's Conclusion.
  - Will have to be written having regard to all the factors worked out during the preparation phase.

YOUR CONCLUSION

'And the point of all that was?'

THE PURPOSE

> The purpose of this section is to ensure you understand the aims and objectives for your Conclusion, that it is the climax of your speech and usually the point at which the ultimate message of the speech is set out.

WHAT YOU NEED TO KNOW

Your Conclusion is the climax of your speech.

It is the point at which what the speech is ultimately about, should come sharply into focus for your audience; where the points that were set out in the Main Body are drawn together to a specific conclusion.

- In the Conclusion of the informative speech, the main message or proposition will be presented or unveiled.

- In the Conclusion of the persuasive speech, the audience will be asked to agree the central proposition of the speech, having been taken through the supporting arguments during the Main Body of the speech.

- In the Conclusion of the motivational speech, the audience will be called upon to take the proposed action, having been told the reasons why the action should be taken during the Main Body of the speech.

- In the Conclusion of the entertaining speech, the audience will be treated to the ultimate (not necessarily the final) punchline or climax of the humour.

By the end of the Conclusion the audience should know exactly what the speech was about.

Since your Conclusion is generally where your overall message will be given or summarised, the Conclusion is also usually the best point at which to flesh out your theme. Here your theme can be used to resonate and imprint the overall message of the speech on the audience, making it the most memorable part of the speech.

For instance, it was in the climactic Conclusion to his 'Yes, we can' speech that Barack Obama actually set out the rallying cry, 'Yes, we can'. It was in his Conclusion that Winston Churchill delivered the rousing words 'We shall fight on the beaches'.

In essence, the Conclusion should be the satisfying completion of your speech. By the end of the Conclusion the purposes of the speech (specific, general and underlying) should all have been achieved.

Using the meal analogy, the Conclusion of the speech represents the dessert that brings the speech to its final delicious peak.

WHAT YOU NEED TO DO

- Understand that your Conclusion:
    o Is the climax to your speech when your overall message is plainly set out
    o Is the point at which the points made in the Main Body of the speech are drawn together
    o Should use the theme of the speech to emphasise the overall message, whether it is to call for a certain action, to persuade towards a point of view, to inform about a certain issue, or simply to bring a climax to the entertainment

- Understand that by the end of your Conclusion:
    o Your audience should know exactly what your speech was all about.
    o Your specific, general and personal purposes should all have been achieved.

YOUR CLOSING

'I leave you with this'

THE PURPOSE

> The purpose of this section is to ensure that you understand the nature and purpose of your Closing, that it is meant to bring the whole speech to an end in a way that satisfies the audience.

WHAT YOU NEED TO KNOW

As your Opening should engage your audience, so the Closing should leave it feeling satisfied.

By now everything that needs to be said has been said, and all that needs to be achieved has been achieved. So, the Closing represents the thing that we as human beings need from a psychological point of view to feel completely satisfied – Closure.

Closure or satisfaction means the audience feels the speech is complete (whether the ending is positive and uplifting, negative and depressing or the countless other feelings a speech can leave an audience with). The point is that the Closing should have a feeling of inevitability – as though there was no other way this particular speech, to this particular audience, on this particular occasion, could have ended.

Think of the end of the classic movie 'Thelma & Louise', with the central characters driving off the edge of the Grand Canyon. As tragic an ending as it was, it felt like the only way the film could have ended after the epic journey the courageous women had undertaken.

Consider the countless romance movies that end with the final confirmatory kiss. The audience already knows it is coming, but somehow the movie is not complete until the kiss has been shown.

Probably the best speech example comes from Martin Luther King's 'I have a dream...' speech, which closes with the famous line, "Free at last, free at last. Thank God Almighty, we are free at last."

As with the Opening, the Closing also provides huge scope for creativity. Options include:

Date references
Location references
Statistics
Humour (a final joke)
Anecdote
Quotation, saying, proverb
Shocker

A good technique is to achieve a degree of symmetry, with the Closing reflecting the Opening, to give the speech a sense that it has come full circle.

For instance, a speech Opening with a date reference could be closed by pointing out some other famous moment in history, that happened in a different year on that same date, and which suggests a slightly different message, or a question posed in the Opening could be answered in the Closing, or a joke could be made in the Opening and another one in the Closing; or a statistic could be set out in the Opening and another in the Closing, etc.

Using the meal analogy, the Closing represents the final digestive liqueur or coffee that rounds the meal off handsomely.

WHAT YOU NEED TO DO

- Understand that your Closing must:
  - Satisfy your audience by ending in a way that feels right and inevitable, in light of the rest of the speech. It should bring closure to the speech.
  - If possible, try to achieve a degree of symmetry by reflecting the Opening of the speech.

YOUR STRUCTURAL OUTLINE

'So, what's the plan?'

THE PURPOSE

> The purpose of this section is to ensure you prepare a structural outline before writing the speech itself. This sets the foundations for a well-balanced and strongly-crafted speech.
>
> It allows you to spot the strengths and weaknesses of your speech before you have actually written it.
>
> It allows you to work out the best order for the points of your speech, plan your timing and identify shortcomings, gaps or problems and work out how to solve them.

WHAT YOU NEED TO KNOW

This is hard work!

Now you have to prepare a structural outline or plan that will serve as the blueprint for your eventual speech. Just as you would not start to build a house without first drafting architectural plans, you should not try to write a speech until you have fully and properly worked out its structural outline.

A structural outline allows you to see the shape, feel and balance of your speech, before it is written.

The fuller and more comprehensive your structural outline, the better you will be able to assess how good your speech will actually turn out to be, and whether it is going to cover all the points it needs to cover to achieve the specific, general and personal purposes for your speech.

Your Structure

Your speech should tell your audience a story, by taking it on an interesting journey from the first thing you say, to the last. Therefore, you have to devise a structure for your speech that allows you to do this.

Every speech will obviously have a beginning, a middle and an end, but more accurately, speeches will generally follow the basic structure of:

- An Opening – the first thing you say to your audience
- An Introduction – the proper beginning of the main part of your speech
- A Main Body – the detail and substance that supports your eventual conclusion
- A Conclusion – the finale/climax of your speech
- A Closing – the last thing you say to your audience

The classic structures for speeches are:

- **Opening**: (the first thing you say to your audience)
  - *Informative, Persuasive and Motivational speeches*: A greeting, quote, anecdote, story, joke, etc.; this is the best place to establish the tone of your speech as your Opening will usually give your audience its first impression of you

- **Introduction**: (the proper beginning of the main part of the speech)
  - *Informative Speech*: A statement setting out the issue or topic that you are going to explain to your audience; i.e., 'The purpose of this speech is to...', or 'How do you solve the problem of...', or 'Today, I'm going to talk to you about...'
  - *Persuasive Speech*: Set out the dilemma/dispute; for instance, a statement of the issue that you are going to try to persuade your audience about
  - *Motivational Speech*: Set out the problem that requires action/remedy

- **Main Body**: (the detail and substance of the speech to support your eventual Conclusion: this is the heart of your speech)
  - *Informative Speech*: Flesh out the information about the subject of the speech with all the main points, supported by the necessary subsidiary points, including references, methodology, statistics, etc.
  - *Persuasive Speech*: Flesh out the main dilemma/dispute at the heart of your speech with all the main and subsidiary points, giving sufficient basis for the view you want to persuade the audience about, with all necessary details

such as case studies, analogies, statistics, etc.

- *Motivational Speech*: Flesh out the detail about the problems that exist with main and subsidiary points; the risks of doing nothing or doing the wrong thing, supported by the necessary justification; examples, analogies, statistics, etc.

You will also have to work out the best order for all the points you will be making within this Main Body. Options include:

- *Order of Relevance* – Often points will simply lead on to each other as a matter of logic. So, for instance, an informative speech about global warming may start with an analysis of the state of the planet now, then contrast that with the state of the planet a century ago, followed by an explanation of the industrial revolution and the consequent pollution and then a projection of the planetary effects if things continue; finally, ending with what steps can now be taken to reverse the anticipated effects in the future.

- *Order of priority* – Make the big points first followed by the less important points; or the other way around, making the lesser points first, leading up to the bigger more crucial points as a crescendo

- *Chronological Order* – Make the points in order of time or date; i.e., the first in time first, leading to the last in time, or alternatively, the last in time first, leading to the first in time at the end

- *Alphabetical Order* – Sometimes, when no other order is logical, something as arbitrary as the use of alphabetical order can work to give the audience some sort of order

- *Problems & Solutions* – The structure involves identifying the problems that the speech is targeted to address, followed by alternative solutions

- o *Causation & Effect* – Set out the cause of the relevant fact or issue, followed by the effect that this issue has had; this can either be with a view to highlighting something good to be celebrated, or something bad, which then needs to be remembered

There is no right or wrong order. It is a question of what works best.

- **Conclusion:** (the finale/climax setting out your conclusions; this is the high point of your speech)

- o *Informative Speech*: Set out the conclusion that you come to after the detail you have gone through in the Main Body; i.e., your answer to the question explored through the speech

- o *Persuasive Speech*: Set out the conclusion you want the audience to come to about the dilemma/dispute, having set out the reasons in the Main Body of the speech

- o *Motivational Speech*: Set out what you want the audience to do to solve the problem that you fleshed out in the Main Body

- **Closing:** the last thing you say to your audience

- o *Informative, Persuasive and Motivational speeches:* Final remark, quote, joke, statement, anecdote, thanks, etc.

Entertainment Speech

Few speeches are exclusively of the entertainment type. This is because whilst a speech might be highly entertaining, it will usually have a more specific purpose, which will still make it an informative, persuasive or motivational type of speech. For instance, a best man's speech is primarily an informative speech (telling the wedding party about the groom), but given in an entertaining way.

So, even if the speech must be entertaining, the speech structure will still follow the structure for informative, persuasive or motivational speeches.

If, however, the speech is meant to be entirely entertaining, then there is no set or ideal structure, it is just a question of what will work to keep the audience laughing.

Your Timing

You need to work out the timings for your speech.

Hopefully, you have already decided on the overall length in both time and number of words. Remember, this is done by taking the length in time of your speech and then working out the number of words at your disposal, by using your word per minute average and multiplying by the number of minutes allocated for your speech. Now you need to allocate timings to the different sections of your speech. So, for instance, where the overall speech length is set at 20 minutes and you speak at 130 words per minute, you might decide:

Opening: 2 mins & 260 words

Introduction: 4 mins & 520 words

Main Body: 9 mins & 1,170 words

Conclusion – 3 mins & 390 words

Closing – 2 mins & 260 words

Total speech time: 20 minutes
Total Number of words: 2,600

The length of time you allocate to each section of your speech should be carefully considered, and will depend on the purposes of your speech. So, if you know the topic of your speech is very weighty and substantial, you may need a longer Main Body, than if your primary aim is to raise the morale of an audience already familiar with the facts, in which case a longer Conclusion may be called for.

If your audience is hostile or indifferent to your message, you may need a longer Opening and Introduction to get it onside, before going into the Main Body of the speech.

Choose Your Best Points

Now is the time to choose the best points out of all the points you identified during the brainstorming stage. Your aim is to pare down all that information to the best 10% of your knowledge on the subject of your speech.

If, during the brainstorming section, you went as far as setting out those points in order of importance, you will already know your best points and these should now be slotted into the relevant sections of your speech.

Your aim at this stage is simply to identify all the points you will make, put them into the relevant sections of your speech and place them in your chosen order, but without starting to actually write the speech itself.

Find The Right Balance

Once you are clear on the points you want to make, your timings and the order and structure of your speech, you now need to find the right balance for your speech.

This involves examining and ensuring that each section of the speech has all the points that it needs, to achieve the purposes of your speech.

If, for instance, you have identified 20 different points to be made in the Main Body of the speech, with each point taking 1 minute to explain, but you have only allocated 10 minutes for the Main Body, this shows you that the speech as you have currently planned it, is unworkable. You must then rework those main points.

Conversely, if you wanted your Introduction to last for 5 minutes (to ease the audience in before getting to the heart of your speech), but you have only identified 2 minor points to be made in the Introduction, this shows that you need to revisit your brainstorming and gather more points to be put into the Introduction.

You should also examine your structure with a critical eye, checking to see whether it works, bearing in mind your purposes (specific, general, personal), the occasion, your audience, your theme, type, tone, and the 'Truth'. Is your Opening structured in a way to make it engaging? Will the points made in the Introduction actually prepare the audience for the Main Body? Will the Main Body have direction, momentum and variety and will it provide the supporting detail you need for your Conclusion? Is your Conclusion the climax of your speech and does your overall message come through with a strong theme? Does your chosen Closing provide a satisfying ending?

This is a qualitative process that involves ensuring that the bones of your speech are well set, so that when the flesh is added (when you come to write the words themselves) it takes on a good form.

Your aim is to create a structure that will take your audience on an easy and rewarding journey, from the first thing you say, to the last.

This is the time for the speech structure to be chopped and changed, torn apart and put back together as few or as many times as necessary, until it feels perfectly balanced.

This is the time to put the work in so that when you come to do the actual writing, you will be able to focus on the words themselves, using the best phrases, most appropriate analogies and interesting quotes, etc., to make your speech come alive.

Make the effort now and you will reap the rewards later on.

WHAT YOU NEED TO DO

- Work out the outline for your speech, bearing in mind the type of speech you are giving (i.e., persuasive, informative, motivational, entertaining).
- Work out the timing and word count for each section of the speech.
- Revisit the points identified during the brainstorming phase and pare them down to the best points to be used in the speech.
- Slot the points into the sections in which they will be used and in the right order, ensuring that you have a sufficient number of points to achieve the aims for each section of your speech.
- Chop and change as often as necessary to get it properly balanced and structured.
- Review the structure to ensure it feels right and will work for your audience and your speech purposes.
- Develop a structure that will take your audience on an interesting journey from the first thing you say to the last thing.

WRITING TOOLS & TECHNIQUES

'Tricks of the Trade'

THE PURPOSE

> The purpose of this section is to show you some of the different writing techniques that can be used to help you write a great speech.

WHAT YOU NEED TO KNOW

There is no one way to write a speech, and no universal standard that works for every speech, on every occasion. The only requirement is that the speech is written in a way that works for you as speechmaker, and for your particular audience.

That said, there are, of course, many tried and tested writing tools and techniques that can be used to enhance and improve your speech. They do not all work for every speechmaker for every speech, but should be used as and when you think they will work for you.

This is just a brief summary of a few examples. For more detail on any particular tool or technique, you should carry out your own research:

Use active and vivid words – Audiences relate more readily to active and vivid words than to passive, dull words. Vivid words evoke clearer images in an audience's mind. Active words, particularly for motivational speeches, move audiences more than passive words. So:

'Excellent' is more interesting than 'good' or OK'.
'Absolutely' is more affirmative than 'yes'.
'We must march' is more persuasive than 'we should go'.
'He did it' connects more than 'it was done by him'.

Alliteration – Repetition of words with the same first letter can be used to emphasise a point, or just give a good rhythmical feel to your words and delivery.

Example: 'She was big, bold and beautiful'; 'The sweet smell of success'

Analogy – This is a comparison between two things that are different, but have sufficient similarity so that the comparison helps to explain, or shed light on, the main point. This technique is particularly useful when dealing with difficult, tricky or complex points.

Sports analogies are common, since a variety of sports have aspects that can be used to support lots of different messages, e.g. team play, discipline, persistence, the virtue of honesty, etc.

On his resignation from the cabinet, Geoffrey Howe famously used a sporting analogy, saying, *"It is rather like sending your Opening batsmen to the crease, only for them to find, as the first balls are being bowled, that their bats have been broken before the game by the team captain."* This was the most memorable passage in his speech, which complained that Mrs Thatcher had been undermining government economic policy on Europe.

Scientists often use the building of Lego houses and structures as an analogy to explain DNA-sequencing. Parables like the story of *'The Good Samaritan'* are analogies.

Anecdotes – This is the technique of telling a story or account of an incident or event (often amusing and personal) on an unrelated subject, but with relevance to the subject or theme of the speech. It is often useful as an intriguing Opening or Closing.

For instance, an economist could begin a speech on economic uncertainty by relating her experience of putting money away for a year, in a piggy bank, to save up for a bike; only to find out that inflation had taken the price of the bike above the level of her savings.

Contrasts – Employing the use of contrasts is a useful means of emphasising a point to an audience, in a way that merely stating the point sometimes does not.

'Not backwards but forwards'
'Out of the darkness into the light'
'Ask not what your country can do for you; ask what you can do for your country'.

I vs You, vs We – If at all possible, avoid talking about yourself too much. Audiences often don't respond well to this. You should restrict the number of times you refer to 'I' or 'me'. It is better to refer to 'you', meaning the audience or even 'we', to give a much greater sense of inclusion.

Imagery, Metaphor, Simile

Imagery is a very powerful tool for painting a vivid picture in the audience's mind, and is particularly useful for highlighting the theme or overall message of a speech.

'I have a dream' – Martin Luther King automatically lifted the imagination of his audience with this direct reference to dreaming.

'Rivers of Blood' – Enoch Powell used extremely striking imagery to describe his doomsday vision of England with the increase in immigration.

'Iron Curtain' – Winston Churchill described the nature and effect of the Berlin Wall and Soviet bloc division.

A *metaphor* involves using a word or phrase to describe somebody or something not literally, but figuratively; e.g., he is a rock (i.e., sturdy and dependable); she is a snake in the grass (i.e., untrustworthy).

A *simile* involves drawing a comparison between two different things to highlight the nature of the thing being described; e.g., he is like a bear with a sore head.

Quotes, Proverbs, Sayings – These are particularly useful as an Opening or Closing and are also a very powerful means of establishing themes. Almost every thought or idea has been expressed by someone else in the past, and probably in a better way. Using familiar quotes, proverbs and sayings (as long as they are properly tailored and relevant to the speech topic) has the effect of helping the audience relate to the speech.

Repetition – Sometimes, to bring home or emphasise a point, a theme or message, simply repeating it is the most effective means. Churchill used it to great effect in his 'We shall fight them...' speech.

Rule of 3 – As a matter of psychology, the human mind relates well to matters being divided into, or set out in three parts. The rule works on the smaller level of 3 words or ideas in a sentence, up to the broader level with 3 main points in an entire speech.

'Father, Son and Holy Ghost'
'The Good, the Bad and the Ugly'
'I came, I saw and I conquered'

Short Sentences – Shorter sentences are easier to understand. You should use an average of 15 words per sentence or less, and make only one point per sentence. This is easier for an audience to digest.

Statistics – Statistics are an extremely useful tool for framing and giving context to a topic through facts with figures.

The key to using statistics is to make them relevant and personal.

Telling an audience that 16,000 children die every day from hunger is certainly capable of shocking, but is almost too grand to truly comprehend. Instead, if you point out that this means one child every 5 seconds, you will have a far stronger impact. Even better, tell the audience that since your speech began, the equivalent of every one of their children had died from hunger and you will see a much greater resonance.

Or, if the statistic is that the earth's diameter is 12,700 km compared with the sun's diameter of 1,392,000 km, you can make this more digestible by holding up a beach ball and a table tennis ball to show the huge size differential.

Secondly, unless it is important to be absolutely specific, it is usually best to round off figures; i.e., 59.8% should be 60%, or 2,988 should be 3,000.

You can use some, all or none of these tools and techniques. It is up to you. The thing is to make sure you write a speech that is right for you and your audience and above all, keep it simple.

WHAT YOU NEED TO DO

- Use any tools and techniques that are natural for you and make the speech easy for your audience.
- Keep to the overriding principle of simplicity.

JOKES & HUMOUR

'Was that meant to be funny?'

THE PURPOSE

> The purpose of this section is to ensure you understand the nature and complexity of humour and how it works in the context of speechmaking; that it is the most technically difficult skill to master, that it calls for very careful preparation, but that used correctly it is probably the most effective weapon in the speechmaker's armoury.

WHAT YOU NEED TO KNOW

Humour done well has huge benefits. Humour done badly will cause you huge problems.

Humour done well gets the audience onside, puts it at ease, breaks up the monotony of a difficult and serious topic and much more. Humour done badly will distract your audience from your main message, disrupt the flow of your speech and possibly alienate your audience. This makes the use of jokes and humour both potentially your greatest weapon and potentially your greatest liability.

There is no definite answer to what makes one joke work and another fall flat. This has been the subject of centuries of discussion and analysis (even Aristotle wrote about the theory of comedy). There are however, certain principles that are generally present in most successful humour, and you should understand them before attempting to use humour in your speech.

- Truth

'Truth' is the crucial ingredient in all humour. It is 'Truth' that resonates with the audience. Think of the best stand-up comic performances and you will note how 'true' the things said are. But, remember that 'truth' in the context of speechmaking is entirely relative. It is what rings 'true' to your particular audience that counts.

Mother-in-law jokes are funny to married people with in-laws, because of the 'Truth' for them that mothers-in-law are difficult, but less funny for a crowd of single people.

- Purpose

Humour must have a purpose. Nothing is achieved by making

your audience laugh uncontrollably, if it comes at a point that requires serious concentration and focus. Equally, a complex and controversial passage in a speech might well benefit from a light touch of humour to keep the audience at ease.

You also have to be clear what level of laughter you are aiming for; i.e., a mild titter from the audience, or a belly laugh. If you are trying to present yourself as a serious and weighty person, toilet humour is not going to help. Humour often works well at the beginning of speeches to warm up the audience, or at the end of the speech to leave the audience with a positive feeling.

Whatever humour you choose to use and when, the point is to use it purposefully and carefully, and not out of a vague notion that it is always good to be funny.

- Relevance

Humour in a speech should also be relevant to the message and purpose of the speech, rather than simply random. It is always possible to make an audience laugh, but if the joke or humour has no bearing on, or relevance to, the subject of the speech, it wastes both time and words – the two most precious commodities in speechmaking.

So, rather than an amusing anecdote about a completely unrelated subject, you should tell a funny story that highlights in some way the theme that will be developed throughout the course of the speech.

This makes the humour doubly potent.

- Audience Analysis

You must tailor your humour to the audience.

Having already analysed your audience, you should already understand what makes it tick, and what it is likely to respond to.

Smutty jokes might tickle a crowd of footballers' wives, but would probably alienate members of the Women's Institute. Elaborate and clever anecdotes might work on lawyers, but would probably bore a group of business tycoons.

- Your Style of Voice

Some people are great at telling jokes, others are terrible. Some have a natural, dry wit, others are more comfortable with slapstick humour. Any humour you use must also suit your natural style of voice. If all forms of humour are simply unnatural to you, consider whether you need to use humour at all.

- Originality

Humour should be original because the best humour feels fresh and new.

Even where (as will very often be the case) a joke or humour is 'borrowed' from other sources, you should always tailor that humour to fit the occasion so that it retains a 'feel' of originality. If you have to use other people's jokes or pre-written passages, you should bend or rewrite as necessary to make them indisputably your own.

It's like the difference between a great cover version of a song, and karaoke. Karaoke is fun to listen to, but it never leaves more than a passing impression on the audience. A great cover, on the other hand, has its own special magic.

- 'Set up' before 'Pay off'

Every joke or piece of humour has a simple two-part structure – 'Set up' and then 'Pay off'.

The 'set-up' is the backstory, the scene that sets the world of the humour.

The 'pay-off' is the humorous completion of that 'set-up' – the punchline or final point.

Speechmakers who struggle with humour tend to do so because they focus almost entirely on working out the pay-off element of the joke or humour; 'What is that funny line that will make them all laugh?' Worse still, they think of the punchline and then proceed to write, rewrite and mould the set-up to fit this contrived pay-off. The result is unfunny.

Jokes and humour work best when the focus is on the set-up, and then the pay-off flows naturally from this, so that it feels like the inevitable conclusion. So, you should concentrate on finding humour in the journey (the set-up) that you take to get to your destination (the pay-off).

- Commitment

For the audience to find something funny, it first has to believe that you are being genuine about it. You have to appear fully committed to your own humour, or your audience will not believe it.

The most important thing is that humour cannot be left to chance.

It must be thought out, planned and executed with care, because there is no lonelier place in the world than on stage with a flat audience, after a bad joke.

WHAT YOU NEED TO DO

- Understand that if you use humour in your speech, it must:
  - Be 'true' from your audience's point of view.
  - Be used for a purpose and not randomly or just for the sake of getting a laugh.
  - Be relevant to the message or content of the speech.
  - Be tailored to your particular audience.
  - Complement your natural style of voice.
  - Be original, or at least rework any borrowed material to make it uniquely yours.
  - Focus on the set-up and allow the pay-off to flow naturally and truthfully out of the set-up.
  - Be committed in a way that lets the audience believe it.

YOUR FIRST DRAFT

'Tell us a story'

THE PURPOSE

> The purpose of this section is to help you write the first draft of your speech. This is not the finalised version, just your first attempt at putting things down. Your sole aim with your first draft is to capture the core and essence of your thoughts for your speech in raw form, which you can then work on during the editing and rewriting stage.

WHAT YOU NEED TO KNOW

So, now comes the moment when you actually write. How do you go about it?

Your speech is the story you tell to your audience. It is a story of the journey from the Opening of your speech (the first thing you say) to its Closing (the last thing you say); from the position your audience starts, (i.e., what it knows, thinks or might do before your speech) to the position you have guided it to by the end of your speech (i.e., what it knows, thinks or will do because of your speech).

Using your structural outline, which hopefully set out your best points in the best order, your aim now is to write down those points in a way that will really connect with your audience. This is where you use your best words and your chosen writing tools and techniques; where you try out the phrases that will make your speech memorable and put flesh onto the bones of your structural outline.

Whereas your outline was just a series of disjointed points, the aim for your first draft is to link all those points together into one coherent and seamless whole, moving (or, as they say, transitioning) smoothly from one point to the next, so that your audience will not feel or sense the joints.

Your first draft will not be perfect. It might not even be close to the text of your finalised version. You are not aiming to get everything absolutely right immediately, but to capture the spontaneity that comes whenever something is said or written for the very first time.

Therefore, when writing your first draft, do it quickly and write it straight through. Use your instincts and write it down in the way it first occurs to you to express yourself. This will often turn out to be the best way.

Do not stop to edit, over-analyse or rethink. Just let your thoughts and words flow and commit them to paper or computer screen. Try to enjoy the process, and let that sense of enjoyment permeate through to the speech itself. So, avoid writing when you are stressed or distracted, or in a bad mood. Instead, lock yourself away for however long you need, turn off the phone and write from start to finish in one go.

If you have gone through the preparation stages as suggested in this book and, in particular, if you have prepared a structural outline already, you should now be chomping at the bit to write, and overflowing with ideas. But, even if you are still unsure, don't worry. Just give it a go and write down what feels right.

By now you should be clear on:

- The 'Truth' you will speak to your audience
- The spirit of the occasion
- The purposes (specific, general and personal) for your speech
- Who your audience is and how best to speak to it
- The type, theme and tone of your speech
- The structure your speech will follow and your best points and the best order in which to make them
- The right length for your speech in both time and words
- The importance of using simple, easy language and being economical with your words
- The objectives to be achieved with your Opening, Introduction, Main Body, Conclusion and Closing
- What humour you want to use; when, why and how

But, with your first draft, you should put those things to the back of your mind, so that they operate on a subconscious level only, and then just write from the heart. Let your instinct be your guide and see what comes out. If a particular phrase or set of words comes to mind, but you are unsure of whether it fits, write it down anyway and carry on until you have fully written that first draft.

The best speeches feel fresh and spontaneous to the audience, and it is your first draft that holds the key to capturing this freshness and spontaneity.

Don't worry about faults or things that you know will have to change. Once you have your first draft, the really hard work will come as you edit and rewrite. That is the stage at which you analyse and assess for 'Truth', theme, tone, humour, etc; when you will chop and change your words and phrases to get them absolutely right, when you will revise and refine every part of the speech until it is perfectly pitched for your audience – all without destroying that initial freshness and spontaneity.

But for now, just write and write from the heart.

WHAT YOU NEED TO DO

- Write your first draft straight through and in one go, without stopping to edit, revise or refine.
- Write with the aim of taking your audience on a journey, by telling it a story that starts with your Opening and ends with your Closing.
- Use your structural outline (if you have done one) as the bones of your speech and write your draft so that it moves smoothly from one point to the next point.
- Put the factors you worked out during preparation (such as 'Truth', theme, tone, spirit of the occasion, etc.) to the back of your mind and write from the heart, focusing on what feels or sounds right instinctively.
- Try to lock yourself away for this first draft and avoid writing it in a bad or stressed mood. Try to enjoy the process and let that sense of enjoyment flow into your writing.

EDITS & REWRITES

'Writing is rewriting'

THE PURPOSE

> The purpose of this section is to ensure that you understand the importance of editing and rewriting, so that you revise and refine your speech to get every single part of it absolutely right.

WHAT YOU NEED TO KNOW

This is hard work.

If writing your first draft is done by instinct and from the heart, rewriting is about using your head and editing ruthlessly.

The aim of your first draft was primarily to write a whole story to tell to your audience and to capture the freshness and spontaneity that all first drafts have. However, for all that spontaneity, your first draft will also be very unrefined, like a rough diamond whose beauty is hidden beneath a rough and crusty exterior.

Rewriting is the art of uncovering, cleaning up and polishing that first draft 'gem' – hence the saying 'writing is *rewriting*'. It is at the rewriting stage that you will refine, revise, break down, reconstruct, amend and fine-tune your speech until every word, every line, every paragraph and the speech as a whole is precisely as it should be.

The key to editing and rewriting is to treat every part of your first draft as dispensable, no matter how beautifully written it appears to be, and however much work was put into it initially. Nothing is sacred. Everything can be changed or discarded. You must have the discipline and courage to throw out anything that you know in your heart of hearts is not absolutely right, and trust in your ability to come up with something better.

Don't be afraid to cut. Consider how you can make every part of your speech sharper and shorter. In particular, think as much about what you should not say (even though during your first draft you were convinced it needed to be said) as what you should say.

This is a meticulous and painstaking process that involves going back over everything, sometimes several times, and reviewing and rewriting from a different angle and focusing on a different aspect each time, until it is perfect.

Ideally, if you can leave some time between your first draft and the editing stage, this will allow you to view your speech as objectively as possible. The aim is to refine the speech without destroying the freshness and spontaneity that was captured at the first draft stage.

In particular, you must ensure that your speech:

Tells the 'Truth' at every point	✓
Follows the so-called 'Rules' where they help, and ignores them where they don't	✓
Complements the spirit of the occasion	✓
Achieves your specific, general and personal purposes	✓
Is uniquely tailored to your particular audience	✓
Is clear on the type of speech it is (i.e., informative, persuasive, motivational or entertaining)	✓
Has a clear theme and overall message	✓

Has a clear overall tone	✓
Contains only the best points, representing the best 10% of your knowledge on the subject	✓
Is the right length in time and words, ideally as short as possible, using an economy of words	✓
Uses simple language that is easy for your audience to hear and understand	✓
Complements your particular style of voice	✓
Is well structured	✓
Uses the best words/phrases and appropriate writing tools and techniques	✓
Contains carefully-crafted humour that is truthful, purposeful, relevant to the message of the speech, tailored to the particular audience, complements your style of voice, is original and focuses on the set-up more than the pay-off	✓
Has an interesting and captivating title that tells the audience what it is about to hear, and sells the speech to the audience	✓
Has an Opening that engages the audience and establishes a bond with it; sets the tone and makes the audience interested in the rest of the speech to come	✓

Has an Introduction that whets the appetite of the audience and leads it into the Main Body of the speech	✓
Has a Main Body that has direction, momentum and variety, and that contains all the points that need to be made to ensure that the purposes of the speech are achieved	✓
Has a Conclusion that brings the different strands of the speech together in a climax, particularly using the theme to emphasise the overall message of the speech	✓
Has a Closing that brings a satisfying end to the speech, in a way that makes sense and feels right and inevitable, and if possible, achieves a degree of symmetry by reflecting the Opening of the speech	✓
Retains the freshness and spontaneity of the first draft	✓
Transitions or moves smoothly from one point to the next to create a coherent and seamless whole speech	✓
Takes the audience on a journey from the Opening to the Closing and tells an interesting story.	✓

Every part of the speech has to work and it must also work as a complete whole.

Your aim, by the completion of your final draft, is to have written a speech that tells the story you want to tell, in a way that will connect with your audience.

Keep every draft of your speech as there will often be something useful from an earlier draft that can be incorporated into a later one.

This is the stage at which your speech actually takes real shape and turns into a living, breathing piece that speaks to other human beings on an emotional level. This is the moment you move from the science and mechanics of the speechmaking process to creating a work of art (which simply means a work that connects with other human beings).

By the end of the rewriting process and after all your hard work, you will have written a great speech.

WHAT YOU NEED TO DO

- Review and rewrite every single part of the speech to make sure it is exactly right, but without destroying the flow and spontaneity of your first draft.

MORE CONGRATULATIONS!

You are now two thirds of the way to giving a great speech.

Whilst the going might have been tough, it has certainly been worth it because, as well as all your achievements from the preparation stages, now you have written a speech that:

- Will appeal to a listening audience, not a reading audience
- Complements your particular style of voice
- Is structured in the best way, bearing in mind the content and your purposes
- Uses simple language with appropriate tools and techniques
- Uses humour properly
- Has a great title
- Engages the audience from the Opening and has a good Introduction
- Flows with direction, momentum and variety in a well-structured Main Body with a well-fleshed out theme, tone and overall message, that tells the truth
- Reaches a good climax in the Conclusion
- Closes in a satisfying way
- Retains the flow and spontaneity of the first draft
- Has been edited and refined to ensure that every part works

Now it only remains to work out the best way to deliver the speech.

Keep going!

HOW TO DELIVER
A GREAT SPEECH

HOW TO DELIVER A GREAT SPEECH

However well prepared and brilliantly written your speech, if it is delivered badly, it will not make for a great speech.

If giving a great speech is like building a great house, your preparation represents the foundations, your writing represents the constructing of the house, and the delivery represents the finishings.

Delivery is what sells the speech to the audience, in the same way that it is the finishings that sell a house to a buyer.

Delivery is where you put colour, flavour and gloss onto the words that have already been brilliantly written.

It is just as critical to the success of your speech as the preparation and writing phases.

A great speech connects with the audience on an emotional level, and the way you deliver your speech is the greatest determinant of how much of a connection you will make.

PASSION

'Say it like you mean it!'

THE PURPOSE

> The purpose of this section is to ensure you understand the importance of putting passion into your delivery. Audiences respond most of all to a speaker that shows a love of his or her subject. They are turned off by a speaker that doesn't.

WHAT YOU NEED TO KNOW

Passion is the single most important quality when it comes to speech delivery. Passion is infectious.

However well prepared and brilliantly written a speech, the audience will not engage with it, if it does not think that you yourself are engaged and passionate about it. But, passion in the context of speechmaking is not necessarily the same as passionate delivery. You do not have to adopt a fire-and-brimstone style of delivery in order to show passion.

What you must show is a personal passion for the subject of the speech, and a total interest and commitment to what you are talking about. This is what resonates with your audience. Like an acting or singing performance, it is when the actor or singer seems completely immersed in the role or the song that the audience is most drawn in. The audience *believes* the performer and so is much more receptive to the content.

So, for instance, the bookworm scientist can display as much passion to her audience when presenting the findings of years of research, as the gregarious army general in a final address to his troops on the eve of battle.

Passion signals to an audience that you are speaking the 'Truth' about your subject.

Passion can be either genuine, (because you genuinely are interested in the subject of the speech) or it can be faked (because you simply are not) – this might be the case when you are called to speak on a subject that you don't really know, or to take a stance that you don't truly believe in. Even in such circumstances, if your aim is to give a great speech, you must still convey a sense of passion to your audience.

The way to show the passion in your speech (whether real or fake) is to:

- Show confidence in and mastery of your subject.

Having brainstormed and researched your speech fully, you should be a master of your subject already. By presenting only the best 10% of your knowledge on your subject, the audience will sense that you know much more than you are showing, and this automatically conveys a sense of your personal passion for the subject. Why else would you know so much about the subject unless you were passionate about it?

- Show enthusiasm for your subject.

  Enthusiasm is infectious. It carries the audience with it. When the audience sees that you are enthusiastic, it will feed off it and become more interested in you and your speech. You have probably experienced this classic situation before:

  Speaker: Good morning.
  Audience: (muted & reluctant) Good morning.
  Speaker: Come on, you can do better than that. I said, 'good morning'.
  Audience: (only slightly louder but still grudgingly) Good morning.

  Why does this method fail? It is because the speaker is trying to force the passion out of the audience, and deep down audiences actually resent this sort of approach. Instead the speakers that generate more interest from their audiences are the ones that seem to have a personal enthusiasm themselves; the ones that genuinely seem to believe it is a great morning, whether anyone else thinks so or not.

  A bad speechmaker delivers a speech in a style that says to the audience, *'You should be interested in what I am saying, even if I am not.'* A good speechmaker delivers a speech in a manner that screams, *'I am absolutely fascinated by this topic. I am so interested and passionate about my subject that I could talk for hours to an empty room about this stuff, and still be happy.*

Hope you enjoy it as much as I do.'

In part, your passion will be shown through the delivery tools and techniques you use (pace changes, pauses, emphasis, etc., all considered later), but mostly this will come from the manner in which you present yourself to the audience whilst giving your speech. Be full-hearted (not half-hearted) about your speech. Don't detract from what you are saying in any way; no knowing winks or subtle gestures that suggest you do not really believe what you are saying.

At all stages you must portray the impression of total belief and commitment to your speech and its subject, even if your personal delivery style is understated and calm.

Once your audience feels your passion, it will be much more receptive to your speech.

<u>WHAT YOU NEED TO DO</u>

- Ensure that you are a master/authority on your speech subject.
- Focus on showing your own personal passion for the subject so that your audience feeds off this, rather than trying to force the passion out of your audience.
- Even if you don't have genuine passion for your subject, fake it.
- Be full-hearted and do not detract from showing total commitment to your speech.
- Use delivery tools and techniques (discussed later) to help you present your speech with passion.

NERVES & FEAR

'You have nothing to fear but fear itself'

THE PURPOSE

> The purpose of this section is to ensure that you understand why you have nerves, and how to master them, and the danger of fear and how to defeat it.

WHAT YOU NEED TO KNOW

Are you nervous? Good. Are you scared? Don't be.

Every speechmaker, from the greatest to the least experienced, gets nervous before giving a speech. Nerves are necessary if you want to give a great speech. Nerves keep you focused, so that when the moment of delivery comes, your senses are at their sharpest. This is the best state in which to deliver your speech. On the other hand, fear is debilitating and obstructive. It inhibits your ability to perform and give of your best.

Therefore, as a speechmaker you should be nervous, but not fearful. Nerves must be mastered. Fear must be defeated. But, how then to achieve this?

- Be confident.

  You have properly prepared your speech (hopefully covering some or all the matters set out in the Preparation section). You have carefully written your speech (hopefully covering some or all of the steps set out in the Writing section). Have confidence then in the speech you are about to deliver, because you have given yourself all the tools you need to succeed.

  Confidence is the natural antidote to fear and the perfect balm to soothe nerves.

  There is no secret weapon to make you confident when you don't truly feel it. You just have to force yourself to act confident, in front of your audience.

  Remember that however nervous you feel, this will not bother your audience, which is only interested in how you give your speech.

- Cherish your nerves.

If you understand and accept that nerves are natural and necessary, this will stop you getting into a panic when those nerves actually come. Nerves are the natural by-product of adrenaline, which surges through our bodies as the biological response when we are faced with an upcoming task or ordeal.

It is adrenaline that gives a man the strength to cut off his own hand to save his arm; that helps a woman with the final push to deliver her baby when all her senses tell her she is spent. It is adrenaline that will give you the fuel for the energy you need to deliver your speech with passion.

- Fear nothing but fear itself.

99% of the time nothing bad ever really happens as a result of bad speeches.

Walls do not crumble; locusts do not fall from the skies, and the earth does not open up and swallow you whole. In fact, the most common consequence of a bad speech is usually nothing more than indifference from the audience and respectfully polite applause. This might be uncomfortable, but it is hardly life-threatening.

A bad speech is usually more of a lost opportunity to make a great impression. But, that is a far cry from the terrible consequences that people about to give a speech, irrationally fear.

In truth, you have nothing to fear but fear itself.

99% of audiences are friendly and want you to do well. Even on the very rare occasions when you are faced with a genuinely hostile audience, and a bad speech really will mean bad consequences, you should still remember that even a hostile audience still wants to hear you give a great speech.

This may sound strange, but it is true. The audience may

violently disagree with the message of your speech, or even hate you personally, but still this hatred does not actually translate into the audience wanting to hear a bad speech.

The reason for this is simple and down to self-interest. No one likes to listen to a bad speech. It is uncomfortable; whereas a great speech is fantastic to hear. However much an audience dislikes or hates a speechmaker, and however much it disagrees with the speechmaker's conclusions, it would still rather hear a great speech than a poor one. History is full of examples of great and successful speeches given to hostile audiences in probably much harder circumstances than you are ever likely to encounter.

So, do not fear your audience, and do not allow fear itself (of giving a bad speech) to become self-fulfilling, so that you actually go on to give a bad speech.

- Get on with it.

    Perversely, the courage you need to overcome an ordeal tends to come afterwards when looking back with hindsight. Unlike the movies, you are unlikely to feel a sudden burst of confidence, following an inspirational pep talk to yourself in the mirror with stirring music playing in the background. Real life is less dramatic.

    Instead you basically have to just put yourself into a positive frame of mind, convince yourself that you are going to give a great speech and then get on with it. It is only when you look back that you will realise you had the confidence you needed all along.

    The positivity of your attitude will become self-reinforcing.

    Equally, if you convince yourself that you are going to give a bad speech, chances are this is what will actually happen.

Focus instead on just getting through the first 30 seconds of your speech, because the start is always the hardest, much like a skydive.

- Use your techniques.

Use whatever techniques that work to help take the edge off the tension that nerves naturally create; steady breathing, a good night's sleep, hearty breakfast, meditation, stretching, physical exercise, a tot of whisky, even the old trick of imagining the audience naked, etc.

Find out what works for you and use it. But, remember that these techniques can only help to take the edge off your natural tension. You cannot rely on such techniques as a substitute for doing all the things needed to conquer your fear and master your nerves.

WHAT YOU NEED TO DO

- Resolve to master your nerves and conquer your fear.
- Be confident in the fact that your speech has been fully prepared and well written.
- Accept that nerves are a natural and desirable part of the speechmaking process and that properly harnessed, they provide the adrenaline needed to deliver the speech with passion.
- Fear nothing but fear itself.
- Think positively and push yourself to just get on with it.
- Remember that your audience wants you to give a good speech – even a hostile audience.
- Use whatever tools and techniques work to relieve the tension created by your nerves.

DELIVERY TOOLS & TECHNIQUES

'It's the way you tell 'em.'

THE PURPOSE

> The purpose of this section is to give you an indication of the delivery tools & techniques at your disposal, to help you deliver your speech in a way that will sell it to your audience.

WHAT YOU NEED TO KNOW

Every speechmaker has a unique style of voice and a unique style of delivery. One person will naturally speak at a brisk and urgent pace; another might be slow and deliberate.

Whatever your style, your aim when delivering your speech is to connect with your audience on an emotional level. You have to make your audience 'feel' what you are saying, in order to reach it.

There is no one way to deliver a speech or speak to an audience. It is a question of what works best given your style of voice, the message, your audience, the venue, etc. That said there are, of course, tried and tested tools and techniques that can enhance and improve your delivery. As always, you should use those tools and techniques that work, and ignore what doesn't.

These are just a very small selection of the various tools and techniques at your disposal. There are many more and you can go into greater depth on each one than is done here. The important thing is to work out what works best for you.

Appearance

Your appearance speaks volumes about you, so you should make sure it says what you want it to say. For instance, if part of your aim is to show your professionalism and seriousness, probably best to avoid dressing sloppily.

If you are speaking to disaffected youths, they may not respond to you if you are dressed stiffly in a three-piece suit.

Of course, there are no rules about this. Churchill gave some of the greatest speeches about the virtues of resilience and the glory of battle, yet his own personal appearance conveyed none of that impression. On the other hand, the simplicity of Ghandi's dress mirrored his uncomplicated speech style and uncompromising message.

Ultimately, it is what is said and how it is said that has the greatest effect on the audience, but you should still be alive to the issue of your appearance, so that it does not detract from the speech, but rather adds to it.

Body Language

Without delving too deeply into the psychology of body language, you should ensure that your general body language is appropriate. Aside from hand gestures, general body language also has an impact on an audience and conveys as much of a message as the speech itself.

It is particularly important to ensure that your body language complements the tone of your speech (that is, the impression you want to convey about yourself to your audience). If you wish to convey a sense of passion and energy, a slouched back and bowed head may conflict with this message. On the other hand, if your overall message is one of sorrow and pain, then flamboyant behaviour may give the opposite impression.

Eye Contact

Obtaining and maintaining eye contact is crucial. It is the surest way to establish a connection between you and your audience.

It has the secondary benefit of allowing you to gauge the reaction to your speech, so you can see whether the audience is interested or bored, clear or confused, with you or against you.

Making eye contact also conveys a sense of authority.

How you make eye contact is up to you. You can do it at selected moments of your speech, or every few sentences. You can sweep your eye across every section of the audience, or pick a particular spot or particular individual within the audience.

The key is to make a connection with the whole audience and keep it through the course of the speech.

Gestures

Some speakers gesticulate wildly and make huge sweeping movements with their hands; others remain completely still and rely on the words to do the work.

Again, it is a question of what works for you and for your particular speech.

The important thing is to be aware of any gestures you make whilst speaking, and to ensure that those gestures do not distract, or detract from the speech, but enhance and improve its delivery and the audience's appreciation.

Intonation

The way certain words or passages are pronounced or phrased, is also another way of adding colour to a speech, to prevent it from being mundane.

Words can be spoken with a vast array of intonations, from singing to nearly robotic, calmly to aggressively, happily to sadly, etc. Points can be accompanied by exaggerated emphasis; others can be underplayed. You can speak loudly to stress certain points, or quietly to draw the audience in closer, as though revealing a secret. You can even shout to be dramatic.

It can help to imagine that the speech is only to be delivered as a voice-over, or over the radio (i.e., where the audience will not in fact be able to see you). All the energy to convey the message of the speech has to go into your phrasing – raising the voice to suggest excitement, dropping it to show seriousness, stretching a word or shortening it, putting on an accent, etc.

All sorts of different levels of intonation can be used to make your words come alive, so that instead of just regurgitating text that has been written down, you are actually delivering it in a way that will connect with your audience.

Pacing

The average speed of delivery of your speech should generally fall between 100 – 165 words per minute. Much slower than this and it can come across as ponderous (although some, like JFK, could get away with this); much quicker than this, and the audience could be lost.

However, within this average, there is significant scope for varying the pace at which certain sentences, paragraphs or whole passages are actually delivered.

Instead of a static, monotone pace all the way through, your speech will capture the audience's interest to a much greater extent if there is some variety to the pace. You can slow down for emphasis, or speed up to convey energy, especially as you move to the climax of your speech.

Pauses

Pauses can also be used either as a general tool all the way through the speech, to give your audience a chance to digest each part, or at specific moments to let the point sink in, or to signal the importance of something just spoken or about to be revealed.

Don't be afraid of the length of pauses. They always seem far longer to you as a speechmaker than to a listening audience. As long as the audience feels that you know where you are going, a pause will not spoil the flow of your speech.

Pauses also often give you as speechmaker, a sense of gravitas and room to breathe and think, just in case you really have lost your place.

How to remember all this

Having decided to use various tools and techniques to deliver your speech, you have to work out how to actually remember to use the right techniques, at the right time and in the right way.

Some, as Churchill did, will mark their texts with every pause, emphasis and pace variation. Others practise to the point of obsession. Some are confident in their ability to simply turn up and deliver the speech instinctively, using the right body language, intonation and eye contact as necessary.

The point is to work out a method (which is probably a combination of notes, intuition and practice) so that the speech is delivered to plan, and not left to chance.

WHAT YOU NEED TO DO

- Use whatever tools and techniques work, to help you to deliver the speech in a way that connects with the audience.
- Work out a plan to ensure you deliver your speech in the way you intend, whether that is by making notes on your text or practising until it becomes second nature.

NOTES OR NOTHING

'Are you writing this down?'

THE PURPOSE

> The purpose of this section is to ensure that you make a considered decision on whether you will use notes, a full script or nothing at all when you deliver your speech.
>
> This section will help you understand the pros and cons of each option, the associated risks and how to protect yourself against those risks.

WHAT YOU NEED TO KNOW

There is no set way to deliver a speech. It is a question of what works best.

Some speechmakers need a full script with every word written down, and notes against every line giving reminders as to pace, pauses, emphasis, etc. Others use notes with bullet points. A rare few use nothing at all.

From the audience's point of view, it makes little difference what option you choose, as long as the delivery is fluent. Your audience won't be impressed that you memorised your entire speech, if it is a bad one. Equally, your audience won't much care that you wrote absolutely everything down, if the resulting speech is excellent.

So, the important thing is to ensure that the method you choose works for you.

Each option has pros and cons, risks and rewards and so you must understand these before deciding which option to go with.

Using Nothing

Delivering a speech without notes or text is very difficult, and something you should only attempt if absolutely confident you can pull it off. It does, however, have great benefits if successfully done.

Firstly, it is extremely impressive and can send a message in itself to the audience – for instance that you are speaking from the heart about a subject of great personal interest to you. David Cameron used this to great effect and acclaim in his bid to become Leader of the Conservative Party.

Secondly, it gives you complete flexibility allowing you to choose words or phrases in an instant, in response to audience reaction. Delivered well, such a speech is particularly impressive, as it has a fantastic air of spontaneity and freshness.

The downside to having no notes or text is the inherent risk of losing your place, or suffering a blank and being unable to recover. This could have a devastating effect on your speech.

In order to minimise this risk, you need to practise the speech delivery fully to make sure you are totally confident, and identify any danger points, where you are prone to making a mistake or losing your place.

You should also pre-prepare a method or technique for getting back on track should the worst happen, and you do go blank. This can be anything from remembering key words or phrases that trigger your memory, to having a set joke to buy time. You could even keep a crib sheet at hand that can be pulled out in such an emergency.

The point is to have a plan that will work to ensure protection from this risk.

Using Notes

The benefit of using notes is that they provide you with a template or skeleton for the speech that can be used to keep yourself on track. The notes can be anything from sketchy bullet points to detailed comments on every single aspect of the speech, but stopping short of a full script.

Unlike the full script, notes only set out the points to be made, as opposed to all the words to be used when making those points.

Notes are the perfect intermediary option for the speechmaker who does not wish to use a full text, but is not confident enough to have nothing at all.

The advantage of notes is the degree of flexibility they provide, because the words of the entire script are not set. Using notes without a set text also makes it easier to change order, or omit entire sections without being knocked off stride, because you are not tied to particular words, which have been crafted in a way that only works if delivered in a certain order.

Having notes provides a readily-accessible structure and means you can concentrate on delivering the speech, rather than trying to memorise where you are headed or what you should be saying next.

The disadvantages with notes is that since they do not set out the words of the speech themselves, but only the points to be made in the speech, there is a risk that you will not say the right words when your speech comes along.

It is also very easy to prepare notes that look fine on paper, but do not actually do the job when the moment of delivery comes – perhaps because there is too much or too little detail.

To avoid these risks it is important to do sufficient practice or rehearsal with the actual notes you intend to use, as this will show you how useful your notes actually are. You will be able to see whether the level of detail is right; that the way and the order in which the notes are written work for you (i.e., whether you prefer cards with large fonts, or scrappy bits of paper with lines linking different points).

There is no set way of preparing notes. As long as they provide the assistance to you that they are designed to, then the form those notes actually take is irrelevant.

Full Script/Text

With a full script/text the speechmaker writes out every part of the speech beforehand, and then delivers it as written.

The benefit of this method is that it allows you to work out your speech in its entirety, before you have actually delivered it, so that you know exactly what you are going to say, and how you are going to say it. You avoid the worry of having to remember anything, or of losing your place or blanking out, but instead can concentrate entirely on how the prepared speech is actually to be delivered.

With the full text you can also go further and annotate every part of the speech, showing and highlighting every pause, emphasis, change of pace, etc.

The risk involved in using a fully fleshed-out script/text is the potential lack of flexibility. It is usually very difficult to break out of the confines of the text of a speech once it is set down, which means reduced scope to change the delivery of a speech in response to audience reaction.

You can protect yourself from this risk by assessing where the danger points in the speech are, and planning possible changes or exit strategies beforehand, that can be used if necessary; i.e., if the audience is not responding to point A, you can quickly move on to point F, without breaking stride. You may also need to be prepared to improvise and ad–lib before coming back to a point in your script.

Whatever option you choose, you must ensure that you will be able to deliver your speech fluently, but with a contingency plan in place for the risks that you can foresee, depending on the method you choose.

WHAT YOU NEED TO DO

- Decide whether you intend to have a full script, notes or nothing at all.
- Write up any notes or script to be used, in a way that will work for you when the moment of actual delivery comes.
- Only use nothing at all, if you are completely confident in your ability to deliver.
- Work out a plan to deal with the risks associated with whatever option you choose.
- Practise fully to make sure your strategy works.

THE VENUE

'Check out the lie of the land'

THE PURPOSE

> The purpose of this section is to ensure that you gather as much information as possible about the venue and how it will be at the time of your speech, so that this can be factored into the way in which your speech will be delivered.

WHAT YOU NEED TO KNOW

Every venue and location is different; whether it is the size of the room, the acoustics, the layout of the stage and seats, where the audience will be sitting, whether there is a stage, podium, microphone, autocue, etc.

Each one of these things will not necessarily affect the content of the speech, but may well affect the way in which the speech is best delivered. For instance, if you are speaking at a venue that is out in the open air, near a busy road at a time when there will be lots of traffic, this will call from a different delivery style than if you are talking in a small, private and intimate room.

If you are in amongst, or very close to the audience, the style of delivery may have to be more intimate than if standing at a podium on a stage at some distance from the audience. If there is no microphone, obviously reaching the audience may require greater voice projection than with a microphone. If there are no IT facilities or equipment, you know you cannot rely on 'Power Point' during your presentation. An autocue may allow you to dispense completely with any notes.

Finding out these details well before the moment of delivery, allows you to plan and adjust the delivery of your speech accordingly, rather than simply being taken by surprise or having to adjust the speech moments before it is to be delivered.

Crucially, it will allow you to factor these things into your practice and rehearsal.

WHAT YOU NEED TO DO

- Get as much detail as possible about the venue for your speech so that you can factor this into your delivery; (i.e., location, dimensions, layout, equipment, etc.).

AIDS & PROPS

'What is the point of Power Point?'

THE PURPOSE

> The purpose of this section is to ensure you understand the nature, benefits and risks associated with the use of visual and other aids.
>
> Aids should only be used if they add a further dimension to your speech and enhance it.

WHAT YOU NEED TO KNOW

Aids (whether visual or otherwise) can be used to great effect in a speech.

Aids and props range from the standard Power Point or Slide Projector presentation to handout notes, film or audio footage, dancers, puppet shows, cartoons, diagrams and charts, props, photographs, etc.

You are limited only by the appropriateness of the particular aid and your imagination.

One of the most famous and effective examples of the excellent use of a prop, came during the actor, Charlton Heston's, speech at the 2000 National Rifle Association convention. Tackling the subject of recent attempts to restrict the use of guns generally, he closed his speech by holding aloft a Revolutionary War Musket whilst proclaiming "From my cold dead hands!" That image and those words came to symbolise the entire pro-gun lobby and indeed became the abiding image of Charlton Heston, even above his many great acting roles.

But, just as aids and props have a great capacity to enhance a speech when used well, they can also detract from, or even destroy a speech when used badly – particularly when the aid is used (as most aids unfortunately are) just because the facility is there.

The only good reason to use an aid is to give an extra dimension to your speech; to present the content of your speech in a different format, recognising that your audience can understand and absorb information in different ways.

If the aid will not do this, do not use it.

For instance, a business presentation full of figures and statistics can benefit from colourful charts and diagrams that present the same information, but in visual/pictorial form. Sometimes, this just makes it clearer.

By far the most common speech aid, and so the most abused, is Power Point. Words in bullet points slide across the screen accompanied by a computer-generated 'whoosh'.

This fancy gimmickry begs some very important questions. What exactly is the point of Power Point? What does its use add to your speech that you cannot achieve with your words anyway? How does it help or enhance the audience's understanding of your speech to see the text bounce around the screen randomly in different fonts and colours?

Bad use of aids distracts an audience and gives it the opportunity to disengage from your speech. Instead of making eye contact with the audience, the speechmaker engages more with the screen, reading out the words as though the audience is incapable of reading! This is not to say aids like Power Point should never be used; on the contrary, Power Point, in particular has a wide range of impressive features, which properly used, can add great value to your speech (even if 90% of Power Point presentations only use about 10% of its features). But all aids should always and only be used for good reason and to good effect.

Far better for instance, to show a short cartoon clip from the Simpsons, which is full of quite profound messages that may be relevant to your speech. Why not perform a trick with some cards to help illustrate some relevant statistics? Or use hand-outs to supplement your words with greater detail than you would want to go into during your speech.

But, first consider whether you need to use any aid at all, or whether you can achieve your speech purposes without them.

If you do decide to use an aid, this must be carefully calculated and planned.

You must ensure that:
- The aid adds an extra dimension to an already well-crafted speech.
- The aid will not distract your audience, or give it an opportunity to disengage from your speech.
- Any equipment is mastered, so that its use is seamless,
- The point at which the aid is used is carefully considered and planned, so that it does not break the momentum of your speech.

As long as your aid will do these things, then it can be a valuable addition to your speech by helping you connect with your audience to a greater extent than just speaking your words might. But, if your aid will not do all these things, then resist the temptation of using and relying on aids, especially Power Point.

WHAT YOU NEED TO DO

- Choose whatever aid you are going to use wisely, ensuring that it will add an extra dimension to the speech by enhancing or deepening the audience's understanding and appreciation of the message of the speech.

- Ensure that the aid will not distract the audience, or give it an opportunity to disengage from your speech.

- Master any necessary equipment, so that its use during your speech is seamless.

- Plan and carefully work out at what points in your speech you are going to use the aid and how you will use it, practising as necessary to perfect its use.

ANTICIPATING PROBLEMS

'Stuff happens!'

THE PURPOSE

> The purpose of this section is to help you understand and accept that your speech may not go 100% to plan. Mistakes may happen; problems may occur. For the risks you can foresee, you should plan some contingencies. For the things you can't foresee, you should put them out of your mind. You will still give a great speech.

WHAT YOU NEED TO KNOW

A great speech is not the same as a perfect one.

However well prepared, brilliantly written and perfectly delivered your speech, there is always a chance that something will go wrong. It might be something big or something small. It might be you making a mistake, or something completely outside your control, failing.

The important thing to be clear on is that such mistakes and problems do not mean that you cannot give a great speech. On the contrary, they provide an opportunity to enhance the greatness of your speech – depending on how you handle it.

You can give a technically perfect speech but one that makes no connection with your audience and this will be a poor speech. Whereas you can give an imperfect, error-ridden speech, where lots of things go wrong, but that still connects with your audience, speaks the 'Truth', complements the spirit of the occasion, etc and this will still be a great speech.

Your audience is not looking for perfection, because perfection is not the measure of greatness. Your audience does not care if mistakes are made or that things do not go according to plan. It just wants to hear you speak the 'Truth' and to feel the passion and sincerity in your delivery. If you give this to your audience and do your best to deal with anything that crops up, your audience will not only forgive and forget any mishaps, it will gain an even better impression of you and your speech, because of your willingness to overcome this adversity, which in itself is an element of greatness.

Far from undermining you, the way you handle any mistakes and problems will enhance your audience's impression of you, and add to your prospects of giving a great speech.

Some problems can be predicted and prepared for; others can't.

The key here is to make a calculated assessment of what the possible risks and problems are, to assess how likely it is that any of these may occur and then to plan a backup or response accordingly.

So, for instance:

- Losing your notes or text – Keep a spare set somewhere.
- Microphone failing – Be prepared to project your voice without one.
- Sweating profusely – keep some handkerchiefs or even a spare shirt nearby.
- Audience heckling – Prepare some stock responses, jokes, anecdotes, etc.
- Change of speech topic – Work out if this is possible and prepare to whatever extent possible, to deliver the speech on this different topic.
- More or less time than expected – (If more time) make sure during the research and brainstorming stage that you really did cover everything, so that you can draw on this information if necessary. (If less time) make sure you are totally familiar with every part of your speech and your purposes, so that you can identify sections or parts that can be dispensed with if necessary.
- More or fewer people – Be ready to adjust the level of intimacy in your delivery.
- Falling over – watch every step.
- Knocking over drink – Clear your speech area of everything.

The lengths to which you should go to plan for these eventualities is entirely up to you, and probably depends on how big a risk you think there is, and how worried you actually are about these risks.

Don't over-worry about what might go wrong, as this in itself could become self-fulfilling and affect your confidence and your delivery.

For the risks that are unforeseen, and thus cannot be planned for, there is only one solution. Don't worry about them. You cannot fix what you cannot help, so don't let the unlikely eventuality of something unforeseen going wrong, affect the way you approach your speech.

Finally, whatever happens, you must take a 'the show must go on' attitude. Trust in the preparation and writing work you have done to see you through whatever crops up, and then just do the best you can in response to whatever happens.

WHAT YOU NEED TO DO

- Assess the possible risks and dangers or problems that may occur.
- Work out a contingency plan to deal with any risks that you are particularly worried about.
- Don't worry about the risks you cannot foresee and adopt a 'the show must go on' attitude.
- Treat mistakes and problems as an opportunity to show your audience how you can overcome adversity.

<u>PRACTICE & REHEARSAL</u>

'Practice, Practice, Practice!'

THE PURPOSE

> The purpose of this section is to ensure that you rehearse your speech sufficiently to make sure it works.

WHAT YOU NEED TO KNOW

Every speech sounds different when delivered, to how it reads on paper.

However well and carefully written your speech, it will always take on a unique dimension when spoken by you and then heard by your audience, and this dimension can never be fully appreciated until the speech is actually delivered.

Proper practice gives you the best opportunity of assessing how your speech will ultimately sound when the moment comes. Practice allows strengths and weaknesses to be identified, difficult passages to be worked on, pace, intonation, loudness, etc., to be judged and fine-tuned.

Crucially, proper rehearsal will also give you familiarity with your speech, which in itself breeds confidence.

The best method of rehearsal is to replicate as closely as possible the circumstances in which the speech itself will ultimately be delivered, and then to practise in that environment.

If the speech can be practised in the venue itself, using the equipment available and with the layout as it will be, even with as much of an audience as there might be at the time, this provides the best kind of practice. Obviously however, some or all of this may not be feasible, so you should simply try to achieve as much similarity as possible.

When rehearsing, you should first practise delivering your speech all the way through without stopping, even when you make a mistake or realise that certain parts of your speech still need to be refined. This is to help you get a sense of how your speech works as a whole, and how it flows from one part to the next. It will also help you identify which passages in your speech are more difficult and so need more rehearsal.

If possible, you should also record your rehearsal, either on video or audio. This will enable you to personally review it afterwards, checking your style of delivery, gestures, intonation, body language, etc. If recording equipment is not available, then use a mirror, or practise in a room with good acoustics (a well-tiled bathroom for instance). The important thing is to try to gain an impression of the way in which you come across and sound, when delivering your speech.

Look out in particular for any ticks and habits that you have and work out whether they are fine for your speech or need to be ironed out. Look out also for your 'ums' and 'ers'.

Practice should also ideally be done in front of an audience, for feedback; i.e., a person or people that can give good, constructive criticism.

In the same way that the editing and rewriting stage of the speechmaking process is used to fine-tune all the elements of the written speech, so rehearsal and practice must be used to fine-tune the different elements that go into the delivery of a speech. So, when practising you should be checking that:

You are delivering with passion.	✓
You have mastered your nerves and defeated your fear.	✓
Your overall speed is not too fast and not too slow.	✓
Your pace is varied to keep it interesting.	✓

Your intonation & emphasis are right.	✓
You use pauses where necessary.	✓
Your gestures and body language are appropriate.	✓
You maintain eye contact.	✓
Any notes or text actually help you when delivering your speech.	✓
Your appearance complements the tone of your speech.	✓
Your chosen aids enhance your speech.	✓
Your speech delivery will work in the venue with the equipment, layout, acoustics, etc.	✓
Your delivery will sell the speech to your audience and help you make a connection with it.	✓

Be careful however, to avoid over-rehearsal.

Just as a speech should not be over-written during the editing so that it loses the spontaneity of the first draft, so the speech should not be over-rehearsed to the point that it becomes stale and loses its edge or freshness.

It is also possible that practice will result in the rewriting of parts of your speech to get it absolutely right, but this should be limited to fine-tuning only, as opposed to wholesale rewriting. If you find yourself doing a substantial rewrite, it means you need to revisit your preparation and writing thoroughly, before again coming back to look at delivery.

Practice is the final stage before actual delivery of the speech.

With proper practice your speech should begin to come alive as you settle into your style. It is at this final stage that all the different constituent elements of your speech come together to create one seamless whole.

This is the last step towards creating your own great speech.

WHAT YOU NEED TO DO

- Practise the speech in conditions that are as close as possible to the circumstances in which the speech will actually have to be delivered.
- Practise as often as necessary to get every part of the speech right.
- Practise the speech all the way through, and then work on the different passages as necessary.
- Record the practice on video or audio if possible, and review to see how the speech comes across.
- Practise in front of people who will give constructive criticism.
- During practice, review the delivery for passion, speed, pace, intonation, pauses, gestures, body language, eye contact, usefulness of notes or text, appearance, usefulness/effectiveness of aids, and suitability of delivery to venue.
- Rewrite & edit where necessary to ensure the speech works when delivered (fine-tuning only).
- Do not over-rehearse.

FINAL CONGRATULATIONS!

So, you have completed the final delivery stage of 'How to Give a Great Speech'.

Having thoroughly prepared and carefully written your speech, you are also now totally confident in how you will deliver it. Now you understand:

- That passion is the key ingredient in the delivery of your speech
- That nerves are necessary and must be mastered; fear is inhibiting and must be defeated
- The tools and techniques you will use to help the delivery of your speech
- Whether to use notes, full text or nothing at all when delivering your speech, the risks associated with each choice and how to protect yourself from those risks
- What aids you are going to use, why and how.
- All the necessary detail about the venue, equipment and circumstances of your speech
- That if things go wrong you can still give a great speech by showing your audience your ability to overcome adversity
- The importance of proper practice and rehearsal

You are now ready to give a great speech!

YOUR SPEECH

There is only one thing better than hearing a great speech, and that is giving one, and this is what you are now ready to do.

You may not have followed all the steps suggested in this book, and there may be things you now wish you had spent more time on. Put that out of your mind. It is a natural and unavoidable feeling to be worried in this way, and probably a good sign that you are taking things seriously. You should be more concerned if you have no worries.

Once the moment of your speech arrives, you have to trust in the work you have done and just get on with it.

You will have nerves, but since you now know how to master those nerves, your aim is to be alert but relaxed.

Above all, enjoy the experience.

Great speeches are meant to be great, not perfect. Your audience is not looking for perfection. It just wants to hear you speak the 'Truth' and feel your passion and sincerity.

My prediction is that your speech will be everything you hoped for and more; that it will touch the hearts and minds of the members of your audience, whether they are adoring fans, tough business clients or harsh and cynical critics; that when you have finished, you will have achieved all the goals you set for your speech, and probably a few more that you dared not even hope for.

Most speeches are forgettable, but yours will be remembered by your audience for some time to come.

Now, take a deep breath, let it out and then go out there and Give a Great Speech!

I wish you the best of luck!

Kolarele Sonaike

GREAT SPEECH.CO
THE 'GREAT SPEECH' CONSULTANCY

CHECKLIST

SPEECH TITLE	
YOUR SPECIFIC GOAL (in no more than 15 words)	
YOUR GENERAL (WIDER) OBJECTIVE (in no more than 15 words)	
YOUR PERSONAL MOTIVE OR AGENDA (in no more than 15 words)	
WHO IS YOUR AUDIENCE? What is your audience's current view of your specific, general and personal purposes?	
WHAT IS THE OCCASION? What is the spirit of the occasion?	
WHAT TYPE OF SPEECH ARE YOU GIVING? (informative, persuasive, motivational, entertaining) Does it complement your Specific Purpose?	

WHAT IS THE THEME OF YOUR SPEECH? What is the one thing you want your audience to remember about your speech topic? Does it complement your General Purpose?	
WHAT IS THE TONE YOU WILL USE FOR YOUR SPEECH? What is the one thing you want your audience to remember about you personally? Does it complement your Personal Purpose?	
TRUTH Have you told the 'Truth' in every part of your speech?	
BRAINSTORM & RESEARCH Have you brainstormed and researched fully, so that you will use no more than 10% of your total knowledge of your subject in your speech?	

HOW LONG IS YOUR SPEECH? TIME: NUMBER OF WORDS:	
WHAT IS YOUR STYLE OF VOICE AS A SPEECHMAKER?	
STRUCTURE Have you worked out the outline structure for your speech?	
JOKES & HUMOUR Is your humour properly planned and truthful? Is it used for a purpose and is it relevant to the message of your speech? Is it tailored to your audience and does it complement your style of voice? Is it original? Does it focus on the set-up journey rather than the pay-off destination?	
YOUR OPENING Does your Opening engage your audience immediately? HOW LONG IS YOUR OPENING?	

TIME: NUMBER OF WORDS:	
YOUR INTRODUCTION Does your Intro lead your audience into the Main Body of your speech? HOW LONG IS YOUR INTRODUCTION? TIME: NUMBER OF WORDS:	
YOUR MAIN BODY Does your Main Body set out all the detail needed to support your Conclusion? Does it have variety, direction and momentum? HOW LONG IS YOUR MAIN BODY? TIME: NUMBER OF WORDS:	
CONCLUSION Does your Conclusion bring your speech to a climax and make clear what your speech is all about?	

HOW LONG IS YOUR CONCLUSION? TIME: NUMBER OF WORDS:	
CLOSING Does your speech close in a way that will satisfy your audience? HOW LONG IS YOUR CLOSING? TIME: NUMBER OF WORDS:	
YOUR SPEECH OVERALL Does your speech feel fresh and spontaneous? Does it tell a story to your audience, taking it on a journey from your Opening through to your Closing? Does it move or transition between each point seamlessly? Will it connect with your audience?	
LANGUAGE Have you used simple language that will sound good to a listening audience? Are your sentences short and clear?	

EDIT & REWRITE Have you gone back through every part of your speech to get it right?	
PASSION Are you going to speak with clear, personal passion for your speech topic?	
NERVES AND FEAR Have you mastered your nerves and defeated your fear?	
NOTES Are you using notes, a full text or nothing at all? What is your contingency plan to address the risks of your chosen method?	
AIDS & PROPS What aids or props are you using? Do your aids or props add an extra dimension to your speech? Have you practised sufficiently to master any aids & props you are going to use?	

VENUE What are the details of the venue (layout, equipment, etc.) Have you factored this into how you will deliver your speech?	
PROBLEMS What are the possible problems that may occur? What contingency plans have you made to protect yourself against these risks?	
REHEARSAL Have you rehearsed your speech all the way through? Have you worked on any difficult passages? Have you reviewed your delivery style to sort out your body language, intonation, pacing etc? Have you practised the different tools and techniques you will use during delivery?	

APPEARANCE What are you going to wear? What message is your appearance going to send about you? Does it complement the tone of your speech?	
YOUR SPEECH Are you ready to give a great speech?	

AUTHOR PAGE

Kolarele Sonaike is a practising barrister based in chambers in Temple, London.

He first attended primary school in Lagos, Nigeria before going on to Kings' School Canterbury in England. In 1994 he graduated in Philosophy & Politics from the University of Birmingham.

After one year, working as a journalist for Newswatch Magazine in Lagos, Kolarele studied law at Westminster University and was then called to the Bar in 1998, since which time he has worked as an advocate, specialising in Commercial Litigation and Employment Law. He is also an accredited Mediator and member of the Institute of Arbitrators.

Since 2006 he has been a Director of the London chapter of the 100 Black Men International Inc, a worldwide charitable organisation that delivers programmes focused on mentoring, education, economic development and health and wellbeing.

Kolarele delivers training on public speaking and speechmaking and also works as a freelance speechwriter. He is the founder of *Great Speech.Co: The 'Great Speech' Consultancy*.

He now lives in London and Lagos with his wife, Eva (founder of Accessories label, *Eva Sonaike*) and their two children.

Made in the USA
Lexington, KY
01 April 2012